'In its broad sweep, this is a most ... a scientist himself, opens with sc ... sciousness and the unconscious, and ... of All Being. Altogether a remarkable achievement and a brilliant response to the New Atheists!'

Owen Gingerich, Professor Emeritus of Astronomy and History of Science, Harvard-Smithsonian Center for Astrophysics, Massachusetts

'In this beautifully written and important book, Russell Stannard provides some answers to the question: "How does one justify a belief in God?" The book is deeply thought-provoking. It should be required reading for theologians, scientists, believers, atheists and agnostics! Evangelical Christians, liberal Christians and humanists will all find their thinking challenged by the insights in this book. It is very clearly written and easy to read, and I have learned much from it myself. This book will be of real value to believers and sceptics alike. I strongly recommend it.'

Sir Colin Humphreys CBE, FREng, FRS, Professor and Director of Research, Department of Materials Science and Metallurgy, University of Cambridge

'Russell Stannard is a master at explaining big ideas in simple prose. He is also one of the world's great communicators at the boundaries of science and faith. So – no surprise – *The Divine Imprint* is a fascinating tour of recent explorations of human nature, theology, and the possibility that God's mind may be revealed in the depths of our own minds.'

David G. Myers, Professor of Psychology, Hope College, Michigan

Russell Stannard is Emeritus Professor of Physics at the Open University. A high-energy nuclear physicist, he has carried out research at CERN in Geneva and at other laboratories in the USA and Europe. He was made an OBE, received the Bragg Medal and Prize from the Institute of Physics and was elected Fellow of University College London. He is a Licensed Lay Minister in the Church of England, a Gifford Lecturer and a Member of the Center of Theological Inquiry, Princeton, USA. A prolific writer for both adults and children, his books are translated into 20 languages and have been shortlisted for many religious and scientific book prizes. He has been a frequent broadcaster on BBC Radio 4's 'Thought for the Day'. His video series, *Science and Belief: The Big Issues*, is currently used by 40 per cent of all UK secondary schools.

THE DIVINE IMPRINT

Finding God in the human mind

Russell Stannard

First published in Great Britain in 2017

Society for Promoting Christian Knowledge
36 Causton Street
London SW1P 4ST
www.spck.org.uk

British Library Cataloguing-in-Publication Data
A catalogue record for this book is available from the British Library

ISBN 978–0–281–07810–3
eBook ISBN 978–0–281–07811–0

Typeset by Manila Typesetting Company
First printed in Great Britain by Ashford Colour Press
Subsequently digitally reprinted in Great Britain

eBook by Manila Typesetting Company

Produced on paper from sustainable forests

Contents

———◆———

Prologue   1

1   False trails   9
Seeking theoretical proof   11
Seeing is believing   12
Filling in the gaps   12
Miracles   14
Argument from design   17
Another argument from design   23
Holy people and holy writings   29
The Ground of All Being   30

2   A new direction   35
Knowing God   37
The conscious God   38
The phenomenon of consciousness   39
The God within   42
The mind: evolutionary psychology   45
The mind: other approaches   104
The otherness of the mind   114
The roots of belief   116

3   Retracing steps   125
The final stage of our journey   127
Why a world?   128
What kind of world?   130
Creation through evolution   145
Evil and suffering   148
Death and eternal life   156
Learning from other people   168

v

Epilogue   171
References   173
Further reading   175
Index   177

Prologue

How does one justify a belief in God? It is a question that becomes particularly pressing as we move ever deeper into what one might regard as a secular age – or, as some refer to it, 'the post-Christian age'. Long gone are the Victorian days when it was the 'done thing' to go to church on Sunday. It was a brave person then who would admit to not believing in God. But all that has now changed. Today those who regularly attend a place of worship are the ones who are in the minority; they are the ones made to feel uncomfortable and odd. Increasingly the use of the word 'God' in public has become a source of embarrassment.

Here I am speaking specifically of the situation in the UK and certain other predominantly Northern European countries. It is not true of the USA – at least not for the time being. There one finds that churchgoing and the ability to speak openly of one's beliefs continue to be the norm. It is no surprise when a Major League baseball player, being interviewed on television after scoring a home run, will declare, 'The Lord has been good to me today.' That is not something one expects to hear from a Premier League footballer on *Match of the Day*! Nor is the USA alone in this. Christianity is flourishing in Africa, and is growing in countries such as Russia and China. How long this will continue is anyone's guess.

But let us return to the countries that are experiencing a decline in religious observance. Why the change? There are probably several contributing factors.

To be frank, in earlier times there was not much else to do on a Sunday other than go to church. In contrast, today the shops are open, there are football matches and cinemas one can attend, and television to watch. There are so many alternatives.

Second, there has been a substantial increase in the general level of prosperity. Health levels have improved and life expectancy has been substantially extended. This doubtless encourages people to feel more self-sufficient and consequently in less need of the comforts and support offered by religion.

But perhaps more important than these, there has been the rise of science – that potent force that daily transforms the way we live. It is not that science is necessarily opposed to religion, as the so-called 'new atheists' such as Richard Dawkins would have us believe. Clashes there have surely been. But these in general have affected only certain forms of religious belief – mainly those based on a literal interpretation of the early chapters of Genesis. The assertion that there really was an Adam and Eve, and that the world was created in six days, inevitably puts one on a collision course with evolutionary theory and Big Bang cosmology. The fact that so many people in the USA have a faith that incorporates such a literal understanding of those passages of the Bible makes one wonder how long such a belief can hold out against the scientific evidence.

But none of these scientific insights affects mainstream religious belief based on a more nuanced understanding of how the various writings of the Bible were meant to be read. No, the impact of science on religious belief has been more subtle than that. It stems from the manner in which the scientific approach is one essentially based on *scepticism*. It effectively says, 'I am perfectly prepared to accept what you are saying, but only provided you can come up with the evidence.' No matter how attractive and aesthetically pleasing a theory might be, it is not to be accepted unless it is backed up by hard, incontrovertible experimental fact – evidence that can be jointly examined and debated. And one has only to contemplate how our world has been transformed technologically by science in the last century to realize how powerfully effective this sceptical approach has been. It is no wonder that this demand for an evidence-based approach has been carried over into other walks of life. One has only to think of the development of the social sciences, sports science, food science, and so on. Hence it appears only reasonable that the claims of religion should be subjected to the same kind of rigorous scrutiny.

But is that so? Is such a mindset appropriate to *all* walks of life? Each time one visits a restaurant, does one demand incontrovertible evidence that the food has been hygienically prepared before tasting

it? Before boarding a plane, does one check that it has been properly
serviced and refuelled, and the pilot is unlikely to have a heart attack?
Prior to marriage, does one demand proof that one's fiancée is going
to be faithful and make one happy? In situations like these, such proof
is not available. Certainly one's actions can be based on sensible, reasonable assumptions – those involving the assumed trustworthiness
of other people. However, there is no prior 'scientific proof' of what
the outcome will be. Strict adherence to the sceptical demand for such
proof before taking action would make life virtually impossible. In
situations such as these, the proof of the pudding, as they say, is in
the eating.

Nevertheless, while fully accepting this to be the case regarding the
choice of the best and most prudent courses of action one might take
in life, and accepting that the adoption of a religious outlook on life
does (or at least, should) lead to profound changes in the way one lives
one's life, it can be argued that there is a prior matter to be settled: does
God actually exist? That is a question seemingly in the category of other
straightforward, unambiguous questions such as: do electrons exist?
Does the Higgs boson exist? Are there planets going round other suns?

Here we have to be careful. Though a question might sound reasonable and in need of an answer, it does not necessarily follow that
it is actually meaningful. For example, on establishing that light had a
wave nature, it was argued that the wave must have a medium (something to do the waving) and this was called the aether. Light travels
through space (from the Sun to Earth, for instance), so space must be
permeated throughout by the aether. The Earth in its orbit around the
Sun must be passing through this aether. Question: how fast is it moving relative to the aether? All very reasonable. Or is it? An experiment
was mounted to find the answer. It failed. Instead it was discovered
that light waves were of a nature that needed no medium; there was
no aether for the Earth to pass through.

Likewise, the question 'Does God exist?' appears at first sight to be
a reasonable one to ask. But note the underlying, unspoken assumption behind this so-called question. It is that God is an existent object
much like any other existent object, such as an electron, a table, a
planet, an apple, and so on. 'God' is just another item that might be
added to the list of existent objects.

But that is emphatically not how theologians regard God. God is not an existent object. Rather, God is to be seen as the *source* of existence. Without God there would be no existent objects. As a crude analogy one might think of an author and his or her books. The author is the source of the books and is not to be confused with what has been written. The German-American theologian Paul Tillich put it well when he declared: God is the Ground of All Being. Instead of asking 'Does God exist?', expecting a straightforward answer 'Yes' or 'No', we ought to be asking whether it is meaningful to think that the existence of the world requires an explanation – an explanation to which we give the name 'God'.

Having said that, there is yet another reason for doubting the wisdom of seeking evidence for God through a sceptical, scientific approach to whatever might be provided by the study of the physical world. It arises from a consideration of the nature of the God whom we seek. How do the major religions think of God? Though there are differences between the religions, commonly recurring themes include a God of love; a God of justice, tempered by mercy and forgiveness; a good God; a God who made us with the intention that we should live a moral life; a God who, according to the Christian faith at least, is a suffering God.

But note: words such as 'love', 'mercy', 'forgiveness', 'goodness', 'morality', 'suffering', and so on, are not to be found in any scientific description of the physical world. Such concepts have no place in the formulation of the laws of nature. Rather, the language used in the description of the world includes entities such as 'electron', 'quark', 'atom', 'molecule', 'cell', and the forces acting between these entities: 'electric', 'magnetic', 'gravitational' and 'nuclear' forces. The language used for talking about God has a much closer affinity with the language used for describing mental phenomena rather than that needed for the description of the contents of the physical world and how they behave. This disjunction does not auger well for our hopes of uncovering God through a scientific study of the world – a study that demands the use of an entirely different language from that appropriate for the description of that which we are seeking. So where does that leave us?

It was while reading Hans Küng's book *Does God Exist?* that I first came across the following quotation from the eighteenth-century German philosopher Immanuel Kant:

> An experience of God is possible, not in the sense that experience
> would make known to me the God whom I could not know without it,
> but in the sense that I can experience God if I already know him.

Ever since I first came across it, I have been mulling over this saying. In fact, it was this statement that triggered the thoughts that led to the writing of this book. Not being a professional philosopher myself, I would not venture to claim that I know for certain what Kant had in mind. But I do know of my own reaction to this statement and the train of thought to which it gave rise.

In the first place it is a very positive statement. It is asserting that there is a God, moreover one who can be experienced. But it appears to discount the possibility of there being a kind of experience capable of proving the existence of God to someone of a sceptical frame of mind – evidence that one might seek through a scientific investigation. In order to experience God there is a prior condition to be satisfied. One has first to get to know this God. But how? How is one supposed to get to 'know' God before one has been presented with convincing evidence that there is indeed such a Being?

That is the question I shall try to address in the following pages. To this end, the book is divided into three parts. First, we shall don the mantle of the sceptic examining the physical world for scientific evidence of God. We shall rehearse the various ways people have tried to prove beyond question the reality of God by such a study – and why all such attempts have failed, leaving the atheist convinced that his or her scepticism of religious claims is justified.

The second part of the book is the important one. It explores what I believe to be the way one can come to 'know' God. There are many different ways people come to a religious belief. It might be because one was brought up in a Christian home, or it might come about through meeting some influential person, or during a time of bereavement, or through Bible study, or when thankful for an unexpected recovery from illness, or when assuming the responsibilities of parenthood, or when facing death, and so on. But these are largely accidentals. They none of them represent the universal core of one's eventual belief. As we shall be seeing, that is rooted elsewhere.

Throughout history there have been theologians who have insisted that the search for God should not begin out there in the physical world. Instead we should be looking inside ourselves. Given that we describe God using the language for describing conscious phenomena, it would seem only reasonable that the search for God should begin through the examination of consciousness.

But if one looks into one's own mind, what does one expect to find there? Surely nothing more than oneself. There are different ways of describing oneself. A physicist will examine our body and account for it in terms of it being an assembly of atoms and molecules held together by physical forces and operating according to the laws of nature. A biologist will account for why that assembly of atoms is the way it is in terms of it having been fashioned over time by evolution by natural selection. The psychologist will give a further description in terms of conscious mental experiences. Each description adds its own layer of understanding as to what constitutes a human being. Accordingly, when one examines the contents of one's mind, what one expects to find there is nothing more than oneself as seen from one of these particular perspectives. That being the case, where is God – the God these theologians claim is found by looking into one's experience of consciousness? The answer, so I believe, lies in posing the following question:

> If this assembly of atoms, fashioned by evolution by natural selection, were to become conscious, what kind of mind would we expect it to have?

As we shall be seeing, our minds in many respects do indeed exhibit the very features we might expect them to have, given the nature of those other more physical descriptions of ourselves. But – and this is the crucial point – our minds have in addition many qualities that are difficult, if not impossible, to account for in such terms. Indeed, in some cases these qualities seem to be the absolute opposite of what we might naturally expect to find in the mind of a self-replicating survival machine – which is essentially how the physical and biological sciences describe us. Furthermore, these additional qualities are found to be the very characteristics we traditionally associate with God. Thus we find our natural animal-type mind appears to have

6

been overprinted by the qualities we associate with God. It is through the recognition of this state of affairs that we come to 'know' God. At least, that is the way I see it. The second part of this book is devoted to setting out what these additional God-like qualities are, and how they come to be there.

The third and final part of the book provides a re-examination of the physical world. This time not through the eyes of a sceptic, but from the vantage point of someone who already 'knows' God and knows what to look for. We shall find that the prior acquaintance with God, gained through the study of consciousness, alerts us to previously unrecognized possibilities of experiencing God through the world. Just as God has imprinted his qualities on to our consciousness, so we find he has imprinted himself on to his physical creation.

To whom is this book aimed? Religious people obviously. It is important for them to be able to justify their faith in a secular age. But not only religious people. Whether one should take belief in God seriously or not is a pressing question for atheists and agnostics alike. To what extent can they justify their *un*belief? Just as in Victorian times most people unthinkingly went along with the generally accepted view that there was a God, now, as I have said, the pendulum has swung in the opposite direction. These days the default position for people who have not given serious thought to such matters is that there is no God. In each case we are dealing with little more than conformity to a herd instinct. Surely, each individual – believer and atheist alike – owes it to him- or herself to take the trouble to formulate for him- or herself a well-considered view on this important issue.

So it is I invite you to accompany me on a journey of exploration – one where we shall be seeking the very foundations of belief – what I call the *roots of belief.*

1

False trails

Seeking theoretical proof

As a preliminary I suppose we ought to begin by asking whether there is a shortcut to belief in God. Without having to call on any tangible evidence, is it possible by merely thinking very hard, to prove logically that there simply *has* to be a God? I have in mind the kind of proof of Pythagoras' theorem: 'The square on the hypotenuse of a right-angled triangle is equal to the sum of the squares on the other two sides.' All of us are happy to accept that this is true. We might not be able to prove it for ourselves. It is many years since, as a schoolboy, I was taken through the proof, and am not sure I could readily reproduce it again today. Nevertheless we all accept its validity. One of the beauties of geometry is that everything is so clear-cut. From a few straightforward assumptions that one is happy to take for granted – such as the shortest distance between two points is a straight line, and parallel lines don't meet – one can prove the theorem to everyone's satisfaction.

It is therefore not surprising that, down through the ages, philosophers and theologians, starting out from a few self-evident statements, have sought an equally convincing proof for the existence of God. Distinguished names figuring in this quest include Plato, Aristotle, Augustine, Anselm, Descartes, Leibniz, Aquinas, and so on.

We shall not spend time going through their various arguments. Suffice to say they failed. Obviously so, otherwise we would all believe in God in much the same way as we all accept Pythagoras' theorem – and there would be no need for this book. But we don't all believe in God. Furthermore, one might add that if such a proof were possible, Jesus would presumably not have come as the son of a humble carpenter, spending his time with ill-educated fishermen, but instead might have been better employed coming as a famous Greek professor, debating the issues with fellow academics and writing books for posterity setting out the proofs of God's existence once and for all. But that, as we know, was not the nature of his mission. He adopted a different approach, and so must we.

Seeing is believing

So let us begin our quest by adopting a scientific approach – one in which we seek experimental evidence from nature for God's supposed existence. It is to be evidence that is available to all, and for which there can be no other explanation than the work of God. That is the line of investigation a sceptic would consider to be the obvious one. We need to explore how far it might take us before perhaps looking at other approaches.

So how does one normally come to accept the existence of something? Through our senses. You believe the book in front of you exists because you can see it. You can feel it and smell it. Indeed, we have become very good at extending our ability in this regard. With microscopes we can see things too small to be seen with the unaided eye. Likewise, the telescope allows us to learn of the existence of astronomical objects too distant to be seen normally. X-rays and other scanning techniques permit us to see right into the interior of our bodies. Such techniques have proved to be a rich source of knowledge.

But, of course, they are of no use in our search for knowledge of God. The God we seek is not one who can be seen, or can be discovered by any of the other senses. We encounter a dead end.

Filling in the gaps

Not that our beliefs about what exists in the physical world are confined to what presents itself directly to the senses. Recall the poem by Christina Rossetti:

> Who has seen the wind?
> Neither I nor you:
> But when the leaves hang trembling,
> The wind is passing through.

> Who has seen the wind?
> Neither you nor I:
> But when the trees bow down their heads,
> The wind is passing by.

It reminds us that we can learn about the existence of things that are in themselves invisible by what we see them doing to things that are visible. The wind is but one example. In the autumn, those trembling leaves fall to the ground. We attribute this behaviour to gravity, despite no one having ever seen gravity – not the gravitational force itself. Like the wind, it is sufficient to see what it does to those things that can be seen. Then there are electric and magnetic forces. We fully accept that they too exist and help shape the world in which we live – a conviction we hold without our ever being able to see such forces directly. It is considered sufficient to observe how a rubbed balloon sticks to one's clothing, or to watch how the needle of a compass moves. Likewise, the place where you are currently sitting is permeated throughout by radio, television and telephone signals borne on electromagnetic waves. In order to demonstrate their existence one observes their effects on the appropriate electronic equipment.

There thus arises the suggestion that perhaps God, though himself unseen, might make his presence known through his actions in the world. Indeed, there was a time when it was felt that God did indeed make himself known in this way, and in no uncertain manner. Thunder and lightning, for example, were regarded as direct manifestations of God's wrath. Plagues and other diseases were regarded as signs of God's displeasure. The coming of rain to water crops was likewise a sign of his blessing. In those days there was so much going on in the world that was not understood. It was all too easy to attribute them to the workings of God.

But then came the dawn of the scientific age. Thunder and lightning were shown to be nothing more than manifestations of electric forces in the atmosphere. Disease was seen to be the work of germs and viruses. The development of cloud physics made sense of weather patterns. Increasingly one came to understand the workings of the world through the formulation of laws of nature. And with this advance of scientific understanding, the gaps in knowledge became progressively fewer. This led to the hope, indeed expectation among atheists, that one day all the gaps would be closed, leaving the so-called 'God of the gaps' with nothing left to do.

A relic of that earlier thinking about God can be found in the wording of certain insurance policies for property damage that exclude 'acts of God' – meaning 'An event that directly and exclusively results from the occurrence of natural causes that could not have been prevented by the exercise of foresight or caution', as a policy I hold states.

One is reminded of a famous comment attributed to the French mathematician and astronomer Pierre-Simon Laplace. When asked where God fitted into his scientific description of the world he replied, 'I had no need of that hypothesis.' Not that this necessarily meant Laplace denied the existence of God, only that God did not intervene in this way.

Miracles

With God being apparently unnecessary for explaining the *normal* running of the world, we move on to ask whether God might be revealed to us through one-off miraculous occurrences.

When speaking of miracles one has to be careful. For a professional theologian a miracle is defined as any event that is specially revealing of God. As such it does not necessarily entail some law of nature being suspended. Indeed, this loose way of referring to miracles is often encountered in daily life. A news item, say, might be about a so-called 'miraculous' escape from a car crash. The newspaper reporter is not necessarily claiming that a Divine intervention has interrupted the normal workings of nature. It is merely a way of describing something astonishingly unlikely. For many the incident is just a matter of luck. There is no need to bring God into it.

What interests us, however, are 'miracles' in the narrower sense of events that would indeed have required a suspension of the normal workings of the laws of nature. Surely this would be evidence for the existence of God. And the Bible is full of accounts of events which, if taken at face value, would appear to be Divine interventions of this kind.

In tackling such miracle accounts it is important to appreciate the mindset of people living in pre-scientific biblical times. In those days, people took a positive delight in tales of wondrous happenings. One has only to examine some of the apocryphal writings that failed to get into the accepted canon to see just how vivid ancient imaginations could be. There is, for example, the story of a man who was turned into a donkey by witchcraft, only to be restored to human form when the infant Jesus was placed on his back. Jesus, as a schoolboy, once made a clay model of a bird, which promptly flew out of the window. Or there was the occasion when a school companion bumped into him, Jesus cursed him, and the boy fell down dead – but happily was brought back to life again by Jesus. Then we have the Apostle Peter engaged in a debate with a magician who impressed the crowd by rising to a great height above the city. Peter called on God's assistance, whereupon the magician fell to earth, was stoned to death by the onlookers – who were instantly converted to Christianity!

All pure nonsense, of course. I suppose it was their equivalent of modern-day science fiction. Good fun, but not to be taken seriously. Nevertheless, the existence of these clearly invented stories that lie outside the writings that make up Scripture does raise the serious question of whether something of the same sort might be going on in the writings that did succeed in being included in the Bible.

An indication that this might well have been the case is the observation that miracle accounts seem to proliferate with time. One can see this if the writings of the New Testament are placed in chronological order – the order in which they were written. They appear in the Bible in the familiar order: Matthew, Mark, Luke and John, followed by Paul's letters. But they were actually written in the order: Paul's letters first, followed by Mark, then Matthew and Luke and finally John.

Paul mentions no miracles – not one – apart from the resurrection of Jesus. Mark, who was next, describes several miracles as well as the resurrection. Matthew and Luke, who both used Mark as a source, include most of those miracles, plus some more of their own. And John's Gospel – the last one – has even more miracles. Put in the order of writing, it does indeed appear that the number of miracle stories might be increasing with time.

Let's take a specific example of the possible generation of a miracle story: Jesus' arrest in the Garden of Gethsemane. According to Mark, one of Jesus' followers cuts off the ear of the high priest's servant. And that's it. He cuts it off. When we come to Luke's later account of the same incident, we find that the ear is cut off, but then Jesus miraculously puts it back on and heals it. A miracle. But if that's what actually happened – a miraculous healing – why no word from Mark about it? Why miss out the punchline? Presumably because, at the time Mark was writing, there was no punchline.

This tendency towards proliferating miracle stories is one reason for being cautious over accepting them at face value. Another is that when approaching one of these accounts, a prior question is whether there might be a perfectly natural explanation of it. Take, for example, the parting of the Red Sea to allow the Israelites to escape from Egypt. It has been suggested that it might have been due to freak weather conditions – a very high wind forcing the water to retreat. Or how about the casting out of devils? That today might be regarded as the work of a good psychiatrist.

Then one has to ask whether the story might have been generated through a misunderstanding of some sort. Take, for example, Jesus walking on water. We read that the disciples are in a boat on the Sea of Galilee and they see Jesus walking on the water. Peter gets out of the boat in an attempt to go to him. Compare that with another story of how the disciples are in a boat when they see Jesus, but this time Jesus is on the seashore. Impetuous Peter again is described as getting out of the boat, this time to swim to Jesus. The two stories are very similar, the only important difference being that, in one, Jesus is walking on the water, and in the other he is walking on the seashore. Biblical scholars have pointed out that if you go back to the original account, written in Greek, one finds an ambiguity. The phrase 'walking on the sea' has another translation: 'walking *by* the sea'. So one has to ask whether Jesus was simply walking *by* the sea – on the seashore – and not on the sea. Has someone, during the telling and retelling of this story, got hold of the wrong end of the stick?

But having said that, not many miracle stories can be accounted for as misunderstandings. So what about all the others?

What we have to note is that there does appear to be a qualitative difference between the biblical miracle accounts and the apocryphal ones. Most of those found in the Bible are not just displays of Divine power performed to impress people, but serve as concrete illustrations of deep spiritual truths. When, for instance, Jesus cures the man born blind, he speaks of the spiritual blindness of the Pharisees who were looking on. At the feeding of the 5,000 he speaks of himself as the bread of life. And so on. We are left wondering whether these accounts were merely stories trying to convey rather abstract spiritual ideas in concrete form, or whether Jesus did in fact perform such actions. One thing is certain. Two thousand years after the event we have no way of deciding the issue in any definitive manner to everyone's satisfaction.

Which prompts us to ask whether miracles occur in our own time. Is it possible to have direct experience of a miracle today? There are many claims that this is so. We hear of people who, after prayers have been offered, or a pilgrimage has been made to a place like Lourdes in France, recover from a condition that had been pronounced by the medical profession as incurable. I know of one such incident myself. But such occasions do give rise to the concern that perhaps there was a misdiagnosis. The condition had not been incurable as originally thought.

One thing is surely true and that is that there cannot be many people, if any, who believe in God purely on the basis of having experienced a miracle. Acceptance of a miracle might well provide confirmatory evidence of one's prior belief in God. We shall have much to say on that subject later. But miracles do not constitute the fundamental roots for that belief. We must move on.

Argument from design

Another attempt at trying to establish God's existence is that based on design. In this regard, the eighteenth-century clergyman and philosopher William Paley is often quoted as pointing out that if you were walking on a heath and you came across a watch lying on the ground, you would immediately conclude from its complicated mechanism and how it all worked together that it must have been designed by someone. Something as intricate as that could not just happen unaided. So, in the same way, he argued, everything about the human body (and the bodies of other animals) is so beautifully fitted to fulfil its function that it must have been designed for that purpose. And that calls for a Designer.

The rug was pulled from under that reasoning, at least as a knock-down proof of God's existence, by Darwin's theory of evolution by natural selection. We shall have need to refer to Darwin's theory many times in this book, so it is important that we should be clear about its main features.

The basic idea is that offspring resemble their parents through sharing the same genetic material. This is in the form of the famous DNA molecule. It consists of a sequence of smaller molecules, the order of which constitutes a code that governs one's physical characteristics. The offspring's DNA is made up from copying those of its parents. However, in the copying process, there are liable to be mistakes leading to variations. There might also be mutations caused by background radiation, which is always present. Some of these mutations give rise to physical characteristics that lead to an enhanced chance of the individual surviving and mating in what can sometimes be a hostile environment. In order to survive we have in mind the need to avoid or defend oneself against predators, the ability to find food, shelter and a mate. In order to meet these conditions, the advantageous characteristics might be the possession of a tough protective skin, sharp claws or teeth, good eyesight and hearing, the ability to run fast, the ability to fly or swim, the use of camouflage as a means of avoiding the attention of predators, and so on. In the case of humans, we have developed a superior intelligence, which has allowed us to find alternative ways of fending for ourselves in a competitive environment. The important point is that the possession of such advantageous mutations to the genes increases the chances of one surviving to the stage where one can mate and pass on those favourable genes to the next generation. Less advantageous or deleterious variations work against the survival prospects of the individual. There is, therefore, less chance of such individuals reaching an age where they can pass on their less effective genes. Consequently, these latter genes have a tendency to die out over time, leaving only the advantageous ones. Whereupon the process is all set to repeat itself, thus giving rise to yet further improvements in terms of survival value in succeeding generations. These incremental improvements progressively build on each other to create the highly sophisticated 'survival machines' we know as humans and the other animals.

The theory of evolution indeed goes further than simply accounting for our physical characteristics and those of today's other animals. There is little use in possessing, for example, sharp claws if you do not know what to do with them. Take, for example, a cat confronted by a bird a little way off. Suppose it did not immediately recognize that it was faced with a potential meal. Instead, it had to painstakingly work out that under those feathers their might be something to eat, and it would thus be a good idea to pounce on it and use those sharp claws to capture and kill it. Such a cat is unlikely to make a kill because, in the meantime, the bird would have flown. On the other hand, a cat that recognized the bird and instinctively pounced – such a cat would be more likely to have a meal, and in the process increase its chances of surviving. There would be great advantage, therefore, in possessing such an innate tendency. And indeed, part of the cat's DNA coding does precisely that: it tells the cat to pounce immediately – without thinking. And that is why today's domestic cat, having had its fill of cat food to the point where it could not eat another mouthful, on seeing a bird in the garden, will instinctively pounce and kill it if it can. We call this tendency *genetically determined behaviour*. Indeed, the animal kingdom offers countless examples of such patterns of behaviour. The way a newborn kangaroo will instinctively climb up the mother's fur and find its way into the pouch waiting to be its new home is but one of countless extraordinary examples one might cite.

Which, of course, raises an interesting question: if we see such genetically determined behaviour in the animal kingdom, and we ourselves are animals who have evolved in a similar manner to them, might not we also be subject to such behaviour patterns? Are we inclined to act without thinking in certain ways? And if so, in what ways? It seems only reasonable to conclude that we probably are subject to such tendencies. We are inclined to adopt behaviour patterns that, for our ancestors, were conducive to their survival. Not that we need regard ourselves as genetically *determined*. To a much greater extent than other animals, we are self-aware. We are able to reflect on what we are doing. There is no need to act as blind robots. We can go against inherent, instinctive behaviour if that is what we decide to do, perhaps in response to some higher demand. Nevertheless, the tendency to behave in the way indicated by our DNA coding will be there. It will take a positive decision on our part to act otherwise. Our behaviour is not genetically *determined*, but there can be little doubt that it will be genetically *influenced*.

Entering the world with already-formed tendencies to behave physically in certain ways, it is only to be expected that our minds will also, to some extent, be pre-programmed. They will exhibit the thought patterns associated with those behaviour traits. We are not born with minds that act merely as blank sheets of paper ready to be written on by whatever experiences we subsequently have. What thought patterns? This takes us into the realm of evolutionary psychology, about which we shall have a great deal more to say later.

So that is the basic idea about evolution by natural selection. It is based on random changes to the genetic material, some being beneficial to its owner and others not. These are then subjected to a systematic selection process whereby the beneficial ones are preferentially preserved for future generations, while the others fall by the wayside.

Actually things can get a bit more complicated than that. What we have to recognize is that what matters most in this process is the survival of the gene. In most circumstances that is synonymous with the survival of the individual hosting the gene. But a mother and her offspring share to a large extent the same genetic material. Under circumstances where it is a case of either the mother or the young being killed by a predator, provided the young are old enough to be able to look after themselves, it is better for the survival of the gene if it is the young who survive. The young can go on and eventually mate themselves, so passing on the gene further. The mother, on the other hand, has already served her purpose. So as far as the gene is concerned, it is advantageous if the mother has built into her a code that compels her, if required, to sacrifice herself for her young. And that indeed is the behaviour we see when a nest is being attacked by a predator such as a hawk. The mother bird is sometimes observed to leave the nest, thus deliberately attracting attention to herself and away from her young.

How far back does the evolutionary process go? It is believed to go right back to inanimate matter. Living creatures developed from matter that was not living.

Which raises the question as to what we mean by 'living'. It is certainly not some magic ingredient that has to be added to the mix. Something is classified as 'living' if it satisfies certain criteria. Among these is the ability to reproduce. To be blunt, living creatures can be described as self-reproducing chemical machines. The copies of themselves that they produce can exhibit random variations from the original. As we have said, it is upon these chance differences that the process of natural selection gets to work, thus producing in successive generations versions of the original that are better adapted to meet the challenges posed by the environment in which they find themselves.

Elaborating further on what distinguishes living from non-living matter, one can add further criteria to be satisfied. There has to be nutrition – the ability to take in substances by way of food to promote the body's functions. One needs to excrete unwanted substances. There must be growth, both in size and changes of shape. Respiration is another requirement, that is to say, the ability to break down complex molecules to provide the energy needed for the body's activities. Finally, one needs to be responsive to the environment.

Ordinary inanimate matter might satisfy one or more of these criteria. Iron responds to the environment by going rusty. Crystals can grow in solution. Chemicals can react exothermally with each other to release energy. It is the *combination* of criteria that defines what is meant by 'life'.

As already mentioned, with this rather mundane definition as to what constitutes life, there is no need of a magical extra ingredient – one that can only have a supernatural origin. This in itself undermines a further argument sometimes deployed in order to justify belief in God. One does not need God in order to account for the existence of life.

The evidence in favour of evolution is strong. There is the fossil record, anatomical comparisons, DNA comparisons and the observation of evolution taking place today (insects gaining immunity from pesticides designed to combat them, being one such instance). Throughout this book we shall be accepting evolutionary theory as having been unquestionably established.

All of which stands against the creationist stance, which holds that man was formed directly and instantly by God in the form of Adam, and that woman was fashioned from a rib taken from Adam's side. This is claimed by creationists as cast-iron evidence for the existence of God – God being the necessary Designer of today's complex biological creatures. But as we have seen, such an argument is countered by the highly plausible alternative offered by evolutionary theory.

A more serious contender as an argument from design is known as Intelligent Design (ID). Unlike creationists, adherents of ID are perfectly happy to accept that evolution has taken place as proposed by Darwin. However, they claim that in the process of going from inanimate chemicals on the surface of the Earth to a fully developed human, there are steps along the way that are so great that they could not have been negotiated alone by the mechanism of natural selection working on random genetic changes. They point, for example, to the formation of the first cell, the appearance of the first multi-celled creature and the formation of complex structures such as the eye and ear. They hold that only by the direct intervention of God could such hurdles have been negotiated. Essentially, ID is a modern form of a God-of-the-gaps type of argument.

One cannot help but have some sympathy for this point of view. There is no doubt that some of these gaps in the evolutionary chain do seem somewhat daunting. And yet evolutionary theorists are coming up with possible scenarios whereby, for instance, something like the eye might have developed. It involves a series of small incremental changes, each of which confers some slight advantage in terms of being able to survive. These then get incorporated permanently into the genetic structure, ready to be further built upon by later advantageous mutations.

Take, for example, the case of the eye. It might have started out as merely a patch of skin that was sensitive to light. A shadow falling on it could be a signal that a predator might be approaching, so prompting an avoidance reaction. But if one is to take flight, in which direction should one go? The shadow by itself does not indicate in which direction the danger lies. For all one knows one might be fleeing straight into the arms of the predator. But what if one's skin were subsequently to develop a dip, and the sensitive patch were to find itself in that hollow? Now, by noting which part of the patch was registering the shadow, one would get a fix on the direction in which the possible predator lies, this prompting an escape in the opposite direction. However, the trouble with a hollow is that it is likely to collect dirt. So it would be a further advantage if a transparent jelly-like substance were to fill the hollow so keeping out the dirt. This jelly in turn could develop into a spherical shape, which would then act as a lens. Now the sensitive patch – later to be called the retina – can register not just a shadow, but an actual image. Now one can see what exactly is causing the shadow. It could well be that it is being cast not by a predator to be avoided, but a potential prey to be chased and eaten. Further elaborations could then consist of a means of reducing the light being received if it is too bright, and increasing it when it is growing dark – hence the pupil. Then there would be yet further advantage in protecting the eye (with eye lids) and washing it when dirty (tear ducts).

This then is one possible scenario by which the eye might have evolved its intricate structure. It is a process involving small incremental changes, each conferring some marginal benefit. Building inexorably on what has previously been achieved, there eventually emerges a sophisticated final product that could not have been formed in one go. That is how the evolutionary scientist argues.

Of course, there is no way of proving that this is actually how the eye developed. We are, after all, talking about possible events taking place long ago, with there being no way of going back in time to verify that they did indeed occur in that manner. That's not the point. What is being offered here is simply one way in which the gaps might have been bridged in a perfectly natural way – one that did not require the intervention of God. How plausible one finds such speculations is up to the individual to decide. I myself find them persuasive.

But one thing is certain: Intelligent Design, as a variant of the God-of-the-gaps type of argument, fails to serve as a proof of God's existence. There is an alternative way of negotiating the gaps. When trying to understand the workings of nature one is surely better advised to seek possible scientific explanations rather than falling back on Divine intervention.

Another argument from design

So far we have taken it for granted that the world we live in is one suitable for the development of life. It had to be or we would not be here. And certainly conditions on Earth are very conducive for life to evolve. However, when we look beyond the Earth, things look very different. The universe is vast. It has taken 13.8 billion years for light to reach us from the depths of space – even though it travels at 300,000 kilometres per second. Those depths are unbelievably cold. The most prominent objects in the sky are the Sun and stars, each star being a distant sun. These are great balls of fire. The Earth is a planet, and certainly there are other planets, but most of them are either too hot or too cold for life, depending on how far they are from their respective suns. Not only that, most do not have the right kind of atmosphere, if they have one at all. The inevitable impression we gain, therefore, is that generally speaking the universe is hostile to life, the Earth being an exception. It is surely not the kind of universe you or I would have designed if we were God intent on producing a home for living creatures.

But we must beware of jumping to conclusions. Things are not what they seem. On closer inspection it turns out that the universe seems to have been at great pains to accommodate us. Indeed, the universe appears to have been fine-tuned for the development of life – an observation known as the *anthropic principle.*

To see what this is about, let me give a brief rundown on how the universe comes to be the way it is. As I am sure everyone knows, it all began with a Big Bang. It was so violent only the smallest atomic nuclei emerged, anything bigger being broken up. So we get essentially just hydrogen and helium nuclei, with slight traces of other elements, together with electrons. As they travelled through space, the nuclei and electrons were subject to an electrical attraction, which led to the formation of atoms. Then, through the operation of gravity, those regions of the hydrogen and helium gases with a somewhat higher density than the average acted as centres of attraction. The gaseous medium, which originally was pretty uniform, became increasingly lumpy. These clumps squashed down and in doing so became very hot (in much the same way as air squashed down in a bicycle pump becomes hot). Due to the resulting violent movements, the atoms split up once more into their constituent subatomic parts. Nuclei began fusing together to form the nuclei of heavier elements, this process being accompanied by the release of vast quantities of energy – the nuclear fusion energy one gets in a hydrogen bomb. This is how a star is born.

Eventually the star will run out of nuclear fuel. It will then no longer have the ability to hold itself up against its own gravity and so collapses. Modest-sized stars then end up as burnt-out cinders. The fate of massive stars is very different. On collapsing, there can be a great explosion called a supernova. This ejects some of the newly cre-ated heavier elements out into space. These can then subsequently come together to form rocky planets circling later generations of stars. Prior to supernovae, the only planets were those entirely made up of balls of hydrogen and helium gas. So this is how the Earth formed. It is essentially a ball of stardust circling the Sun – the Sun itself being a later-generation star. The scene is now set for evolution to take over and produce life – a lengthy process taking 4.5 billion years before we humans put in an appearance.

It all sounds pretty straightforward. Except that it is anything but. Take, for example, the violence of the Big Bang. Had it been any less violent than it was, the mutual gravity acting between everything would have eventually brought the expansion to a halt. With grav-ity still operating, everything would from then on start coming back together again. This would lead to a Big Crunch, all this happening before life could have enough time to develop. Alternatively, had the violence of the Big Bang been any greater, everything would have been flung apart so rapidly that all the material would have dispersed before it had time to collect together to form stars. And without any suns there would again have been no life. In other words, the violence of the Big Bang had to be just right – and it was.

What matters here is the density of the matter coming from the Big Bang. If the density were greater than a certain value it would be Big Crunch; if it were less than that value it would be a case of expansion for ever. The borderline case is known as the critical density – a dens-ity that would give an expansion that eventually came to a halt, but only in the infinite future. So what is the actual density? It turns out to be exactly the critical value. A coincidence? Not really. Scientists have a good explanation for it. They believe there was initially a period of exceptionally fast expansion called inflation. And it is the nature of this special type of expansion that ensured that the density ended up with the critical value. This solves the problem of how we come to have such a fortuitous rate of expansion, but in turn raises its own kind of question: why should the start of the universe have incorpor-ated a process like inflation? Who ordered that?!

So much for the expansion. How about the strength of gravity? Make it any weaker than it is and the temperature rise on squashing the hydrogen gas down will not reach the 1 million degrees necessary to light the nuclear reactions. That would mean there would not be any suns. As we have already said, no suns means no life. On the other hand, make gravity stronger and you will, of course, get stars, but now one has so much gas squashed down that one gets only giant stars. Such stars have more fuel at their disposal than a medium-sized star like our Sun, so one might think their fires would last longer. In fact, the reverse is the case. The squashing becomes so pronounced that they reach higher temperatures, and that in turn leads to the fuel burning much faster. The result is a larger, but short-lived star – one incapable of supporting the energy needs of evolution on a nearby star for the lengthy time required. The evolution of intelligent life takes so long that it can be successfully accomplished only if served by a slow-burning star like ours – a medium-sized star produced by the kind of gravity operating in this universe. So in order to get life, the strength of the gravity force needs to be what it is.

As for the production of the heavier elements in stars, even that is not as straightforward as one might think. In particular, there is a problem in getting carbon to form. Carbon is essential for the subsequent building of molecules of biological relevance. But it would seemingly require three helium nuclei to stick together, and getting three nuclei to collide at more or less the same time is as difficult as getting three billiard balls to collide simultaneously. Two colliding yes, but not three. Fortunately the three helium nuclei do manage this trick, thanks to what is called a nuclear resonance. How big one moving nucleus appears to another can depend on their approach speed. At certain speeds there can be a resonance such that the target nucleus looks exceptionally large and so is easier to hit. And that is exactly what happens in the process whereby three helium nuclei fuse together to form carbon. First, two of the helium nuclei collide to form an unstable form of beryllium. Then, because the resulting nucleus looks large to an approaching third helium nucleus, they are able to collide and fuse before the beryllium has a chance to spontaneously break up. Thus we get carbon. And it was all due to that fortuitous resonance. Or was it just fortuitous – a coincidence?

Then there was the slight problem of location. It was all very well producing the heavier elements by nuclear fusion, but where are they? They are in a star at 1 million degrees – hardly a suitable environment for evolution to take place. They have to be got out into space. As we have just seen, that was done by supernova explosions. But how can an *im*plosion caused by the attraction of gravity lead to an *ex*plosion? The mechanism of supernova explosions remained a mystery for a long time. It has now been solved satisfactorily. The material is blasted out by a burst of subatomic particles called neutrinos. Neutrinos are well known for hardly interacting with anything. They can pass quite easily right through the Earth from England to Australia without hitting any of the intervening matter. And yet it was these elusive particles that ejected all the material that goes to make up the Earth and our own bodies. What a relief they were not even more elusive.

What else? Well, there is the matter of how many spatial dimensions there are in this universe of ours. One would think that a universe could presumably have any number of spatial dimensions. Ours has three. And that was lucky for us. It is only in a space that has three dimensions that planets can have stable orbits. Perturb the orbit of the Earth somewhat and it is no big deal; it simply settles down into another nearby stable orbit. But with additional dimensions that would not be the case; there would be no stable orbits. And without orbiting planets able to keep a safe distance, while at the same time being warmed by the Sun, evolution would not be possible.

We can sum up this discussion by saying that the universe, far from being hostile to life, has seemingly bent over backwards to accommodate us with a whole string of . . . what shall we call them? Coincidences? Nor is this list exhaustive. Indeed, the closer one examines the structure and working of the universe, the more one realizes just how conducive it is to the production of life. As indicated earlier, this state of affairs is called the anthropic principle.

How are we to account for it? Was it in fact consciously fine-tuned by some agency with us in mind? Certainly, on the face of it we seem to have been handed the father and mother of an argument for the existence of a Designer. So is this the knock-down proof of the existence of God we have been seeking?

The short answer is No. There is an alternative interpretation: the *multiverse.* This is the suggestion that our universe might not be alone. There might be others – a great many others – perhaps an infinite number of others. They all exist in parallel with each other. The whole ensemble is known as the multiverse. All of these individual universes are envisaged to be running on different lines, each with its own characteristic values for the strengths of the forces, the masses of its constituent parts, and so on. In the vast majority of these universes there is no life because one or more of the conditions necessary for its development are not satisfied. It is only in the very occasional freak universe that all the conditions, purely by chance, happen to be met. It is only in these that life is able to get a hold. We ourselves, being a form of life, must obviously inhabit one of these freak universes. That way there is no mystery about the universe matching our needs so exactly.

Naturally it is hard to see how one could ever verify the truth of the multiverse hypothesis. Other universes, by not being part of the known universe, almost by definition are unobservable. I say 'almost' because there could be an exception. A variant of the theory is that the multiverse, instead of being made up of absolutely separate parallel universes, might consist of a space broken up into different zones, each zone being a bubble universe. If this were the case, it would appear to raise the possibility that one might be able to move from one bubble, across a dividing boundary, and into the neighbouring one. By travelling out into space sufficiently far we might come to such a boundary separating our universe from our neighbour. We would then be able to prove that there were indeed universes other than our own, and that the laws of nature and other basic physical characteristics were different from our own.

The trouble with this idea, unfortunately, is that the continuing expansion of the universe is carrying these other universes away from us so fast we would never be able to catch up with any of them. So it looks as though the multiverse idea, even if true, is never likely to be verified. This has led many scientists to claim that the multiverse hypothesis should be regarded as belonging to philosophical speculation rather than genuine science.

Not that that need worry the sceptic demanding proof of God's existence. Recall that the object of the exercise we are engaged in at present is that of seeing whether the believer can provide unambiguous proof for the reality of the Divine. The sceptic has merely to propose a possible alternative. The anthropic principle, no matter how persuasive it might strike some people, cannot be counted as incontrovertible proof of a Designer God. The sceptic has the get-out option of putting his or her faith in the multiverse instead.

Holy people and holy writings

So far we have concentrated on examining the physical world – its contents, its workings and its origins. We now change tack. Inanimate physical objects are not the only things to which we have mutual access. We can also make observations of fellow human beings. For many people their belief in God is not at all based on trying to account for the behaviour of the physical world. Instead it is based on acceptance that Jesus was the Son of God; it is through Jesus one experiences God. Muslims look more to Muhammad. Jews have Moses and other great Old Testament leaders and prophets. Central to such faiths are holy writings such as the Bible and Qur'an, setting out the lives and teachings of such figures. Some would go so far as to claim that these writings are the very word of God.

There can be no doubt that contemplating the lives and teachings of holy people, as set down in Scripture, does for many act as the route by which they come to take religion seriously. For this reason they are of paramount importance, and we shall be elaborating on that later. But do any of these approaches constitute the very ground on which belief is based? The answer must surely be No. One does not *have* to be a Christian in order to believe in God. One does not *have* to be a Muslim or Jew, and so on. Today's great world religions can be regarded as alternative approaches to understanding the spiritual realm, each coloured by differing histories and cultures, each with its own distinctive insights. Moreover, we note that ancient people believed in God (or gods) long before today's religions were established. Such believers had no access to the teachings and examples of those we revere today, and yet they would surely claim to be as much open to the Divine presence as ourselves. The age into which one is born, and the culture to which one belongs, seem largely immaterial when it comes to the ability to establish a relationship of some sort with God. Thus the particular religion to which one belongs, with its specific spiritual leaders and writings, cannot be the universal, fundamental roots of belief that we are seeking.

In short, if not all spiritual believers accept Jesus as the Son of God, why should the sceptic? If not all spiritual believers accept Muhammad as the great prophet appointed by God, why should the sceptic? We conclude that the study of our fellow human beings, no matter how exceptional some of them might be, is no more successful at proving the reality of God than the study of the physical world.

The Ground of All Being

We have been talking about the nature of the world, what it contains and how it is run according to the laws of nature, its apparent design, and so on. But all of this leaves out of account an all-important prior question, namely: 'Why is there anything at all?'

Some might attempt to answer the question by pointing to the Big Bang. That was how the world came into being. But why was there a Big Bang? Who or what was responsible for it? The religious believer might be inclined to answer: God. Everything that happens has to have a cause, and God was the cause of the Big Bang. Without God the world could not have got started.

At first sight that sounds like a promising argument in favour of the existence of God. But again we find ourselves going down a blind alley. There are alternatives to the God hypothesis.

For example, in his book *The Grand Design*, Stephen Hawking puts forward a rival proposal. He suggests there might be a law of nature, the function of which is to produce universes out of nothing. It created this universe and presumably many others. In anticipation that this law exists, he calls it M-theory.

At first it might seem impossible that something could arise out of nothing. But not so. Take, for example, electric charge. It comes in two forms: positive and negative. In high-energy collisions between subatomic particles it is commonplace to produce electric charge. The trick is to create as much positive charge as negative charge. That way the *net* charge remains the same. It is the net charge that is important.

Indeed, the net charge of the entire universe appears to add up to precisely nothing.

The same goes for other physical quantities such as momentum – a property of moving objects. One can push a stationary object and produce momentum where previously there was none. But again one can only do this if one at the same time produces an equal and opposite momentum in whatever is doing the pushing. So, for instance, in order to fire a bullet – thus giving it momentum – the gun must recoil with an equal and opposite momentum. Or from standing still, you can only start to move and gain momentum by pushing with your feet against the ground and in the process sending the Earth recoiling in the opposite direction (just a little!). With as many things moving in one direction as another, one finds that, like electric charge, the net momentum in the universe is zero.

Even matter can be accounted for in this way. Matter is known to be a form of energy. It is the transformation of matter into other forms of energy – heat and light – that keeps the Sun's fires burning. But we know that energy itself can be both positive and negative. Two objects, such as an atomic nucleus and an electron, when bound together by their electric attraction for each other, have less energy than when they are apart. We can see this in that it takes energy to prise them apart. This addition of energy – positive energy – is necessary to overcome the negative binding energy of the combination. In the same way, each object in the universe is subject to the gravitational attraction of all other objects in the universe. It is thought that these gravitational forces might be producing enough negative binding energy overall to completely compensate for all the positive energy manifest in the movements of matter and in the stuff of which matter is made.

Indeed, a plausible case can be made that the entire contents of the universe add up to precisely *nothing*! Thus all that is needed is a means of rearranging this nothingness into the more interesting form of nothingness that constitutes ourselves and what we observe in the world.

It is this rearrangement of the initial nothingness that is the supposed function of M-theory. But even if there were to be such a theory (and one needs to emphasize that there is no evidence for it whatsoever), would this really provide the way forward? Would it not in turn raise the question as to why there is an M-theory? Why is M-theory in charge rather than some other theory? Indeed, why is there any theory at all? Would not the existence of an M-theory point to the existence of God – a God who set up the theory?

Leaving aside the suggestion of a possible M-theory, let us return to the question of what else might have caused the Big Bang. Can a case be made that it needed a Creator God to get it started? The problem with this is that the Big Bang was very special. It was not like other explosions. Other explosions, such as fireworks going off, occur at some point in space and at some instant in time. But according to physicists, the Big Bang did not occur at some point in space. Rather it saw the coming into existence of space itself. Space started out as an infinitesimally small dot – no space at all – and with the expansion of the universe, it has been growing ever since. Not only that, it is claimed the Big Bang saw the coming into existence not only of space but also of time. The reason for this is that in Einstein's theory of relativity there is a very close connection between three-dimensional space and one-dimensional time. In fact, they are regarded as being indissolubly welded together to make up a four-dimensional entity called spacetime. One cannot have space without time, nor time without space. So if space came into existence at the instant of the Big Bang, there is a powerful reason for believing that the same was true of time; it also came into being at the Big Bang. There was no time before that instant. And that in turn means that there was no cause of the Big Bang. Cause has to come before effect, and here the effect is the instant of the Big Bang. So any cause would need to precede in time that instant. But there was no such time then.

There is actually nothing particularly new in this idea. The fourth-century theologian St Augustine had concluded long ago that time was as much a property of the world as any other, and would therefore have had to have been created along with everything else. He did not, of course, have access to an argument based on our modern understanding of relativity theory. He did not need it. He simply argued that we can only know about time through the movement of objects. We speak of the objects as changing their position in time – the hands of a clock, for instance. But if there were no objects because they had not been created yet, the concept of time would have had no meaning. So when Augustine thought of a Creator God he certainly did not have in mind a God who existed for all time and at some point in that time decided to make a universe.

Basically we have here a classic confusion between two terms, 'origins' and 'creation'. Although these terms might be used interchangeably in ordinary everyday conversation, in theological discussions they take on specific and quite distinct meanings. Origins is all to do with how things get started – how they originated. This is a topic that holds very little interest for theologians. Creation is distinctively different. When theologians speak of God the Creator, they have something else in mind. They are asking about the very source of existence. If nothing existed, would that call for an explanation? No. Why should anything exist? But as soon as something exists, then the questions arise. What is responsible for certain things existing and not others? To what do we owe the fact that we are existing at this instant? Theologians are not especially interested in any first instant. For them the Creator is as much involved in the present instant as any other. Creating a universe was not just about getting it started and then leaving it to get on with things unaided. The world had to be sustained in existence. That is why God is described not just as the Creator of the world but also its Sustainer. Everything that exists is timelessly dependent on God.

The question as to why there is something rather than nothing has exercised the minds of philosophers and theologians down through the ages. Some incline to the view that the question is meaningless. And certainly, as we have already noted, when one is addressing deeply philosophical or scientific issues, occasionally the way forward is to recognize that the question one is asking, though it makes good grammatical sense, actually is a non-question. We saw this earlier in the attempt to measure the speed of the Earth as it passes through the (non-existent) aether. The question was meaningless. In a similar vein, there are thinkers today who dismiss as meaningless the question concerning why the world exists. The world is there, and that is all one can say on the matter. One just has to accept its existence as a brute fact and get on with the job of science, which is to describe it.

Others accept the validity of the question. They accept that it is a perfectly reasonable question and that it deserves an answer. And the answer is God. God is the name we give to whatever is responsible for existence. Descartes took as the starting point for his philosophy: 'I think, therefore, I am'. He might have added the further truism: 'I am, therefore there is a God who created me.'

So does this need for a Ground of All Being constitute the very roots for belief in the God that we have been seeking? Of all the attempts we have been making to establish a foundation for belief in God based on our observations of the physical world, this is probably the most likely candidate. But does it provide proof? The answer yet again has to be No. Certainly there can be little problem accepting that there might be some kind of source responsible for the phenomenon of existence. But why should this source have to be the kind of God one does in fact believe in – a personal God who takes a conscious interest in each and every one of us, a God who loves us and possesses all the other qualities traditionally associated with God? Why not some blind, inanimate pseudo-physical creative force or agency of some sort? If there is to be a further truism to be added to that of Descartes, perhaps it ought not to be: 'I am, therefore there is a God who created me', but rather, 'I am, therefore there is that which created me.'

No, the time is long overdue for us to face up squarely to the kind of God we are seeking, and what that might imply for our search for God.

2

A new direction

Knowing God

Let me remind you of the quotation from Immanuel Kant that got me thinking on this subject:

> An experience of God is possible, not in the sense that experience would make known to me the God whom I could not know without it, but in the sense that I can experience God if I already know him.

As I have indicated, this somewhat enigmatic statement really sums up the entire message of this book, though that will take some unpacking!

It is a statement that offers hope that there are indeed experiences that testify to the existence of God. However, they are not of the sort we have so far unsuccessfully been seeking – evidence that compels belief in God. Rather, the kind of evidence on offer is of a nature that confirms what one already accepts. But that, of course, immediately raises the question of how, in the absence of objective proofs of God's existence, one comes to 'know' God in the first place. What might persuade, or indeed compel us to drop the sceptical approach we have so far adopted in favour of a more positive approach? I repeat: how does one get to 'know' God?

What is certain is that Kant did not mean 'know' in the sense of having a complete understanding of God. One might master one's multiplication tables and hence know that 3 x 3 = 9. But one does not have that kind of knowledge of God. Countless theologians down through the ages have asserted that God in that sense is completely unknowable. No, what we have in mind here is a different meaning of the word 'know'. We are using it in the sense of being acquainted with someone. You might be asked, for example, whether you know the people living next door to you. By that one does not expect you to know everything about them. Rather, you are being asked whether you are at least on speaking terms with them. Do you know their name? That sort of thing. An ancient use of the verb 'to know' is 'to have sexual intercourse' with someone. That, of course, is the ultimate way of getting acquainted with someone – without it necessarily implying that one knows anything at all about the other person in the other sense of 'know'.

The same holds true of the use of the word 'know' in the context of God. Kant did not mean having knowledge or understanding of God. Having explored attempts to find the kind of convincing evidence that leads to acceptance that there is a God, he concludes, 'I have therefore found it necessary to deny *knowledge* to make way for *faith*.' It is clear that one cannot have knowledge of God in that sense, but only in the sense of being acquainted with God.

Closer to our own times, the celebrated Swiss psychologist Carl Jung was once asked in a television interview whether he believed in God. He replied, 'I know. I don't need to believe. I know.' Again we have the claim that it is possible to know God in this latter sense. But in the apparent absence of any clinching scientific evidence, how does this conviction arise?

The conscious God

Earlier we noted that the language we use in describing God is not that which is employed for the description of the physical world. For instance, if one were allowed just one word to describe God, what would it be? That word has to be 'love'. On being asked which was the greatest commandment, Jesus replied:

> 'You shall love the Lord your God with all your heart, and with all your soul, and with all your mind.' This is the greatest and first commandment. And a second is like it: 'You shall love your neighbour as yourself.' On these two commandments hang all the law and the prophets. (Matthew 22.37–40)

This God of love has a purpose in mind for us: he wants us to behave in certain ways and not in others. A distinction is drawn between good and bad behaviour. God wants us to enter into a relationship with him. He offers hope in time of trouble, for example. Furthermore, Christians believe in a God prepared to suffer on our behalf.

But as we earlier pointed out, words such as 'love', 'purpose', 'wanting', 'good', 'hope', 'suffering', together with a host of other terms such as 'joy', 'despair', 'fear', 'making a decision', do not figure in scientific descriptions of the physical world. They do not appear in physics equations. Physics has no need to refer to such things. Neither does biology. The biological description of humans and other living creatures deals with cells, chemicals, the flow of blood, the flow of electrical signals in nerves, and so on. Such descriptions make no use whatsoever of the kind of terms we need to use when describing the type of God we seek. When speaking of God, the language needed is that commonly used when describing *conscious experience.*

That being the case, does this not throw into doubt the wisdom of beginning the search for God with a consideration of the physical realm – a study that inevitably relies wholly on the use of terms none of which apply to that which we are seeking? Surely our search has got off on the wrong foot. If so, you might ask, why did we begin our investigation with the physical world? Simply because we are children of our time. It seemed the natural thing to do. We live in an age of unprecedented scientific progress in the fields of physics, chemistry and biology. The focus has been on the properties and behaviour of matter. This has resulted in consciousness taking a back seat; it has been neglected, or even ignored as an inessential epiphenomenon. But it did not have to be so. In the past, many, indeed most classical philosophers chose the study of consciousness as their starting point, rather than unthinking matter. It was argued that the only thing one can be sure of – absolutely sure of – is the contents of one's mind. Everything else, including even the existence of the physical world and our interactions with it, are but hypotheses for trying to make sense of conscious experience. Understanding what goes on in the mind is ultimately what it is all about.

So it is we set aside our consideration of the physical world – for the time being at least. It is a subject to which we shall return in due course, once we have, through our study of consciousness, got to 'know' God. Only then shall we be in a position to acquire the necessary perspective for recognizing the confirmatory evidence for God made available through that physical world.

The phenomenon of consciousness

Consciousness is a mystery. By that we do not mean a puzzle awaiting a solution. We are using the word 'mystery' in the sense of something that is likely always to lie beyond human understanding. It faces us with the recognition that human knowledge has fundamental limitations. That does not stop writers from time to time claiming to have solved the problem. One thinks, for example, of the American philosopher Dan Dennett's book *Consciousness Explained* (1991). But none of these attempts has been convincing. And I suspect it will remain that way.

So how can one begin to come to terms with consciousness? Each of us can only speak with certainty of one's own experience of it. I know I am conscious; I have mental experiences. Of that I am certain. But what else can I be certain of?

Those mental experiences of mine make me aware of the physical world. In particular, I note that a specific feature of that physical world – namely my physical body – seems to have a close connection with my mental life. If the body sustains a cut, I feel pain. Put things in the mouth and I experience a taste – sometimes pleasant, sometimes not. It depends on what I am eating. Taking certain pills relieves a headache. Lower the temperature of the body and I feel cold. Warmth, on the other hand, is accompanied by a feeling of comfort. And so on.

This raises the question as to whether other features of the physical world are also accompanied by mental experiences – experiences of their own. A worm, for instance. Cut it in half and it writhes about as though it is in agony, as indeed I would if I had, say, a finger cut off. But one notes that both halves of the cut worm are writhing about. So what does that mean? Both halves are in agony? Does it now have two minds whereas previously it had only one? Or does it not have a mind at all?

How about a fish? I know what I would feel if I had a hook stuck in my mouth. So is the fish also in pain? We appear to be assuming that it is not, or that the pain is not significant, for otherwise angling would presumably have been banned. The truth is that we simply do not know what, if anything, a fish mentally experiences.

So how about something easier? What about other humans? My observations of the physical world reveal bodies very similar to my own. Knowing the close connection between my body and my mental experiences, it is only natural to assume that these other bodies will also be accompanied by analogous mental experiences. These other bodies have brains like mine, and I know there is a link between my brain and my conscious experience. Electrical signals travelling along nerves in my body to the brain are associated with various mental sensations. I observe that these other human bodies behave in the same way with the passage of electrical signals to their brains. Presumably they too produce analogous mental experiences in their minds. Not only that but these other human bodies talk and claim to be conscious. The conscious experiences they describe resonate with those that one experiences oneself. It is therefore a reasonable assumption to make that these other bodies are indeed accompanied by their own minds – far more reasonable than to assume they aren't. To claim to be the only sentient creature in the world would be absurdly egocentric.

And, of course, the acceptance of minds other than one's own radically alters how one views the world and how one behaves in it. The recognition that other people are not just intricate arrangements of unfeeling inanimate chemicals, but are likely to experience love, pain, hope, fear, joy and so on, enormously enriches one's appreciation of the totality of existence and how one should treat other people, to say nothing of other advanced animals.

All of which sounds very reasonable and straightforward. Except that I have no proof – *absolutely no proof at all* – that anyone, apart from myself, is conscious. Let us be clear: everything about the physical actions of other people can be explained in a fully self-consistent manner using purely the language of the physical sciences. We have seen how Laplace, in his description of the physical world, declared that he had no need of the hypothesis of God. I imagine if he had been asked about what role consciousness played in his scientific equations, he might well have added that he had no need of that hypothesis either.

And yet despite finding that the physical world provides no scientifically verifiable proof of the existence of the consciousness of other people, we have, nevertheless, been trying to find evidence in the physical world for a conscious God – a Super Consciousness, if you like to call it that. If studies of the physical world and its workings are incapable of offering incontrovertible proof of the consciousness of other people, it is clear that applying such an approach to finding evidence for the consciousness of God was doomed from the outset.

The God within

If one is searching for a conscious, personal God, then it seems only logical that one should begin with an examination centred upon the phenomenon of consciousness. That should have been our starting point; not, as we have so far assumed, the physical world. Rather we should have been asking ourselves what we know about consciousness – what experience of it does one have?

As I have already said, I myself have direct experience of my own consciousness – the contents of my own mind. And that is all. You are subject to the same kind of restriction. You can access nothing but the contents of your mind. (Here, of course, I am giving you the benefit of the doubt and assuming you do have one!) Hitherto we have been looking outside ourselves for evidence of God. Changing course, we now look inwards.

There is nothing new about this change of outlook. St Augustine put it well when he said of God: 'Late have I loved you . . . You were within me and I was outside, and there I searched for you . . . You were with me, but I was not with you.' He was not alone in directing attention to one's innermost being rather than the external world. The seventeenth-century philosopher Blaise Pascal said: 'It is the heart which perceives God and not the reason.' He went on to talk about 'a God-shaped vacuum in the heart of every man which cannot be filled by any created thing, but only by God'. The fourteenth-century monk and theologian St Gregory Palamas declared that God was not to be known through created things but through direct experience of God through the heart. He held that we must empty the mind of everything else in order to find God within.

But how? Surely, one might think, if one looks into one's own mind, all one will find there is oneself! As we have already noted, what is offered there is an alternative, inward perspective on oneself to that gained by a physical examination of one's body from the outside. Let me repeat: there are various ways of describing what it is to be oneself. There is the physicist's view of us as an assembly of atoms and molecules subject to the laws of physics. The chemist sees us as a collection of chemicals undergoing chemical reactions. The biologist sees us an evolved animal. The psychologist regards us as one who has mental experiences associated with the brain. And one might add that the theologian sees us as a spiritual creature relating to the Divine. Each level of description has its own insights to offer as to what it is to be human. No single description is reducible to the others. Though physics might be regarded as the most fundamental of the sciences, it is simply not true to say that once one understands everything that goes on at the atomic level one has a complete description. It would be arrogant for the physicist to claim that chemistry and biology are reducible to physics. At each of the higher levels new concepts come into play – those that are called emergent properties. We see this even within the discipline of physics itself. Take, for example, the properties of pressure and temperature. These parameters describe the overall average behaviour of an ensemble of atoms. Where would weather forecasting be if one could not refer to high and low air pressure systems, or what the temperature was likely to be? Yet these properties do not even exist at the level of the individual atom. If we can see these new properties emerging within a single discipline, how much more common is it likely to be as one moves from one discipline to another?

Although emergent properties offer us new insights as to what is going on, nevertheless they have to be understandable and consistent with what is going on at the lower level. Air pressure, for example, is a measure of the amount of momentum (i.e. mass multiplied by velocity) being transferred to the surface of the Earth by the air molecules. Momentum is indeed a property of an individual atom. But what the individual does not possess is an *average* momentum; that has to be the characteristic of an ensemble of atoms. In the same way, we think it useful to distinguish between living and non-living matter. But what do we mean by this emergent property called 'life'? As described earlier, it really involves a combination of features such as nutrition, respiration, responsiveness to the environment, excretion and reproduction. It is the combination of the full set of properties that is important and leads to our recognizing that a new feature has emerged. But as I have said, the new feature must be understandable

43

and consistent with the lower-level description, in this case the description of the various component features.

In the same way, although the psychological description of ourselves upon which we are about to embark will not be reducible to the descriptions of ourselves given by physicists, chemists and biologists, it must nevertheless be consistent with what is going on at those other levels.

And so it is we turn our attention to the psychological description of ourselves. We examine the contents of our mind with the aim of seeking the elusive evidence for God. We do it in order to get to know God. But as already pointed out, this raises an obvious question: how might an examination of something that is nothing more than one's own mind lead to our getting to know God? On examining the mind, what do we find there?

Before embarking on that quest, though, a brief word as to what is to come. Although this is a book about belief in God, in the next 50 pages or so there will be no mention of the word 'God'. You might start wondering where all this might be leading! So as to orientate you, the plan we are following is set out here.

On examining the contents of the conscious mind we find traces of all that has ever happened to us in the course of our lives so far: memories of past experiences, knowledge we have gained, character-forming lessons we have learned, personal detail after personal detail. All these are exclusively to be found in the mind of the particular individual. As such, they are of no interest to us in the context of our search for God. Forget about them. Instead, we concentrate on a second feature of the mind – one we all share. This concerns the way all of us, from the moment we are born, come into the world with minds that are not blank; they already have a structure of sorts to them, leading us automatically to think and feel along certain well-defined lines. This arises from the way our evolutionary past has left its imprint on the brain we have inherited from our distant ancestors, and consequently its thinking.

But that is not the whole story. There are inborn characteristics of the mind that are difficult if not impossible to explain in this manner. How do these latter characteristics arise? I will be contending that God, as the source of *all* existence, is to be seen not only as the

44

source of the physical world, as we have already discussed, but is also the source of consciousness. Our consciousness derives from God's consciousness. That being so, it would seem reasonable to anticipate that our minds, by their very nature, will in some respects incorporate features characteristic of the mind of God. Indeed, we shall be finding that those innate qualities that are difficult to account for in terms of our evolutionary inheritance are in many respects the very features we have traditionally come to associate with God. Truly, as it says in the Bible, we are made in the image of God. Yes, our evolutionary past has left its indelible imprint on our minds, but so also has God. It is the aim of the following pages to try and disentangle the two. It is by isolating those contributions attributable to God that we get to know him. That at any rate is the plan.

No easy task. Evolutionary scientists have already achieved much in accounting for features of our inborn mental characteristics and are making further progress today. Deciding which additional features might be open to explanation along these lines, and which others lie outside that sphere of competence and require some other type of explanation, is bound to be controversial. Hence the rather lengthy, but I hope interesting, discussion upon which we now embark.

The mind: evolutionary psychology

The medieval philosopher and theologian Thomas Aquinas held that there is 'nothing in the intellect which was not previously in the senses'. In other words, at birth the mind starts out as a blank slate upon which subsequent experiences are to be written. Moving closer to our own times, this same stance has been incorporated into much of the thinking of the social sciences. What some people call the 'standard social science model' holds that the mind does indeed start out essentially as a blank. It might have a few innate generalized abilities that can subsequently be applied to a range of problems, but there is no specific content to them. More or less everything has to be learned by the individual. The culture we are brought up in is what moulds who we become. It is society that shapes us. Society in its turn, so it is claimed, has been shaped by what it was in the past. As we shall see, though seemingly reasonable, this viewpoint has come in for heavy criticism.

An alternative approach is to note that the mind is especially associated with what is going on in the brain. So let's begin by looking at the structure and function of the brain. It is a physical system that operates something like a computer. It is carbon-based rather than made up of silicon chips. It is composed of neurons that are cells specialized for the transmission of information. Electrochemical reactions cause the neurons to fire. Neurons are connected to form circuits much like those to be found in computers. These brain circuits are connected to neurons extending throughout the body. Some of these neurons fulfil the function of collecting sensory information from outside. Take, for instance, those signals coming from neurons associated with the retina of the eyes. The circuits process this information so that what is presented to the conscious mind is not the raw data of a pair of two-dimensional pictures, one from each eye, but a three-dimensional object. This construction of a three-dimensional image is not something we consciously have to work out each time. It is automatically done for us by the way the brain has been constructed. Additional specialized circuits process the information contained in air pressure differences detected by the ears. The recognition of different sounds, and the direction from which they are coming, is again done automatically. In addition to the neurons associated with gathering sensory information, others that extend throughout the body are connected to the muscles and cause them to activate. Hence, in response to the sensory information gathered from the environment, the body undergoes movement. In this way the brain governs behaviour and the mental processes that go with those physical actions.

These innate characteristics can go far beyond the simple automatic processing of visual stimuli from the eyes to form three-dimensional visualizations, or the instinctive perception of the direction from which sound is coming based on the signals coming from the two ears.

Here we enter a field of study known as *evolutionary psychology*. Though Darwin himself recognized that the evolutionary process would not only shape our physical characteristics but also our minds, evolutionary psychology did not really get going as an academic discipline in its own right until the 1930s and 1940s. Evolutionary psychologists, while accepting that the culture into which one is born and raised does indeed influence how we develop, nevertheless maintain that we come into the world with many brain circuits, each adapted to meet quite specific problems that our ancient ancestors faced. With there already being set patterns in the brain at birth, then we must expect that there will be set patterns to the way we think. Though it is true that culture helps shape who we become, these inborn psychological tendencies we all share have, in their turn, helped shape culture.

Evolutionary psychology is based on three assumptions. First, just as we come into the world as an evolved animal with certain innate genetically influenced behavioural characteristics – characteristics that are universal for all humans – so in the mental sphere we should expect that there will be a common psychological nature.

Second, the genetically influenced behaviour patterns were honed as adaptations to recurring problems posed by the environment – problems that in some way were related to reproduction and the passing on of genes. They were concerned with such factors as the need to find food, shelter, a mate, and the ability to avoid predators. We would therefore expect that our pan-human psychological nature would parallel those concerns. Just as the physical body has developed a variety of features, each adapted to deal with some specific problem, so the mind has a modular structure where each component has been fashioned in response to meeting a specific challenge. Whereas some psychologists regard the mind as a kind of all-purpose central processing computer, evolutionary psychologists prefer a model whereby the mind is likened to a whole array of mini-computers, each adapted to deal with some specific problem.

In this respect the mind has been likened to a Swiss Army knife with its collection of tools (scissors, nail file, corkscrew, bottle opener, knife blades, magnifying glass, not to mention the thing for getting stones out of horses' hooves), each dedicated to meeting a particular need. Just as it is easier to assemble a wide range of individual tools rather than try to devise some ingenious device capable of dealing with all problems, so it seems to evolutionary psychologists that it was more likely that the mind over time would have evolved a range of simple input/output mental devices, rather than a single, flexible, comprehensive, central computer capable of handling any problem it might confront.

Finally, we have to bear in mind that when we think of adaptive behaviour we are not necessarily talking about behaviour in our modern-day world with all the challenges that can throw up. Evolutionary change is a slow process, particularly if one has in mind the evolution of complex structures. Humans spent some 2 million years, or 100,000 generations, as Pleistocene hunter-gatherers, a few thousand in a civilized society, and only 100 or so in the technological age. Whereas we instinctively avoid snakes and spiders, which might be poisonous, are repelled by the smell of rotting food and experience vertigo when venturing too close to the edge of a cliff – all hazards that have been around for ever – there has not been enough evolutionary time for us also automatically to avoid touching exposed electrical wires or to look both ways when crossing a busy road. These latter survival techniques have to be learned during the span of one's own individual life. Indeed, our innate abilities have probably not even had time to adapt to an agricultural type of life.

No, when we talk about our innate behaviour patterns and common psychological characteristics, we are almost exclusively talking about the ways in which Pleistocene people had to respond to the challenges thrown up by their need to hunt animals and gather plants in the African savanna. This accounts, for example, for the well-established difference in the spatial abilities of the sexes. Males have a superior ability, this arising from their role as hunters in the Pleistocene epoch – a role that required navigational skills used in tracking down prey and cutting off their retreat, and finding one's way home if one has had to go far in pursuit. Females, on the other hand, have an innate advantage when it comes to remembering objects they have seen and their locations – a skill that arises from their traditional role as the gatherers of plants for food. They have to recognize which plants are edible and where in their surroundings they have been found in past excursions. Unlike prey, plants don't move but are often partially hidden in complex vegetation; and it can require a specific skill to identify them.

Some of these inborn mental characteristics are so basic we tend to take them for granted. There is, for instance, from the age of ten weeks, a clear understanding of what an object is; that is, it is a bounded something that occupies space and is continuous in time. Its solidity means no two objects can occupy the same space. Another example is the recognition of which events are causally connected and which are not. Then we note that young children can make the distinction between animate and inanimate objects, this being based on the idea that living objects are self-propelled in their movements whereas the non-living only move when acted upon. This, of course, is not invariably true, but is a useful criterion as a rule of thumb.

Yet another example is the distaste that one can have over having sexual relations with a sibling with whom one has been raised. Given that mating with close relatives can often lead to birth defects, this is again a useful trait to have.

We are born with an ability to recognize faces and to discern from facial expressions and body language what emotions the other is experiencing.

We have an innate ability to master a language. Not any specific language, of course, but a generalized readiness to learn a language of some kind when introduced to one. Here we are specifically referring to spoken language – not necessarily the ability to read or write. It is believed that the acquisition of language ability was a slow process whereby genetic variations gradually led to increasing competence. Each component, as it emerged, led to some evolutionary advantage for our ancestors in that it allowed for communication at a more sophisticated level. The use of language made it possible to learn from the experience of others rather than having to learn everything from one's own personal involvement. In this way language became a feature throughout the human population, to the point where we now come into the world pre-programmed ready to handle highly subtle and complex sentence constructions. Children as young as three years are able to be quite fluent in their use of complicated grammatical sentences – all this without being formally taught such skills.

A point to bear in mind is that not all inherited traits are directly related to the adaptive solution of some problem. There can be by-products – properties that are coupled in some way to an adaptive function, but that of themselves do not convey any additional evolutionary advantage. These are sometimes known as *spandrels*. The word 'spandrel' is an architectural term referring to the roughly triangular space between the tops of two adjacent arches and the ceiling. One finds them, for example, in cathedrals, where the barrel-vaulted nave and transepts meet, forming four arches separated at the top by spandrels. These spaces are often painted with religious scenes. That being the case one might be tempted to ask why the artist chose a triangular shape for his painting rather than the traditional rectangle. The answer of course is that the artist did not have any special reason for choosing a triangular configuration. The shape of the picture was dictated by conditions that had nothing to do with artistic preferences.

In the same way, when dealing with some inherited characteristic we must not automatically assume that it has to be an adaptation to meet some specified problem. It could well be nothing more than an indirect by-product of something that was a genuine adaptation. To be recognized as a spandrel it must be possible to identify the functional adaptation to which it is related and show how the coupling has come about. So, for instance, bones are functionally adapted in that they lend rigidity and strength to the architecture of the body. But the fact that bones are white does not confer any additional advantage. The whiteness just happens to be a property of the chemicals that make up the bone, mostly calcium salts.

Again, as we have seen, there is advantage to be had in being ready at birth to learn a language and thus able to communicate with other people. This was originally done by the spoken word. Later came the development of writing. But that was not because there was additional survival advantage to be had specifically from writing. The ability to write is just a by-product of what really matters: the ability to master a language. Likewise, there is little if any survival advantage to be had from engaging in modern-day sports such as football and athletics. We might be good at such activities, not because our ancestors living in the African savanna played games, but the skills exercised in sport, such as strength, fast running, being nimble, are to some extent the same as those that made our ancestors successful hunters.

Not all of these inborn abilities date back to the Pleistocene epoch. Language acquisition, for example, is a comparatively late development. It has happened since hominids split off from the other great apes. But that is an exception. Most of our innate characteristics were gained in the distant past. It is strange to realize that, lurking in the deepest recesses of our mind, there is an ancient person from a long ago different age from the one we are living in today!

Not all of these traits manifest themselves at birth. Interest in sexual relations does not become apparent until later. The manner in which a woman takes to being a mother is another feature that comes into its own as an adult. Because these attitudes are not apparent at birth they might lead one to think that they must be absent at that stage and have had to be learned from the culture in which one has been raised. But this is not necessarily so. In such examples, the evolutionary adaptations we have acquired are there from birth, but for a while lie dormant awaiting the circumstances encountered later in life when they can to advantage take effect.

In summary, evolutionary psychologists hold that we have a vast number of innate characteristics, each fashioned in response to our ancestors adapting to some specific demand repeatedly posed by the environment. We definitely display a certain amount of flexibility when tackling new problems. However, this is not thought to be due to some generalized skill divorced from any specific content. Rather it is thought to arise through our calling simultaneously on a range of specific skills, it being the combination of these skills that gives rise to the perceived flexibility when tackling novel situations.

Thus the mind from birth has a certain built-in architecture and, so far at least, we have satisfactorily been able to account for it in terms of it being the kind of mind we would expect to be associated with the brain of a self-replicating survival machine operating in accordance with the laws of nature. For that is the description of ourselves as seen from a purely physical point of view. Francis Crick, the co-discoverer of the genetic code wrote: 'Our highly developed brains, after all, were not evolved under pressure of discovering scientific truths but only to enable us to be clever enough to survive and leave descendants.' The sociobiologist Edward O. Wilson puts it like this: 'Knowledge of the world ultimately comes down to chemistry, biology, and – above all – physics; people are just extremely complicated machines.'

According to those who subscribe to this materialist philosophy it should be possible to explain not just those features of the mind we have so far discussed, but *all* the innate characteristics of the mind as being those expected of such a machine. But is this the case? This is the important question.

In what follows we shall explore further features of the mind. Unlike those we have considered up to now, these appear to pose problems for this line of reasoning. Though evolutionary psychology will be seen to have further successes in accounting for the innate nature of the mind, as already mentioned, other aspects of mental experience will be more difficult, if not impossible, to explain away under the assumption that we are *nothing but* survival machines. And if that is the case, we must ask how such an additional input might have been made. How could such extra patterns of thought and feelings have got into the very structure of the mind?

Awareness

According to a materialist philosophy, consciousness is of secondary importance. It is something that just happens to run in parallel to what really matters, namely what is going on in the physical brain. It is dismissed as an *epiphenomenon*. It is affected by, indeed caused by, the primary phenomenon: the brain processes. The interaction between brain and mind is one-way; the brain governs consciousness; consciousness is incapable of affecting the brain.

Furthermore, physical objects such as the brain slavishly obey physical laws. Cause is predictably followed by effect. When it comes to trying to account for what is going on in the world, consciousness plays no part. The mind is wholly circumscribed by the nature of the physical object that has given rise to it, namely its brain, and the brain in turn is blindly following the dictates of the physical laws.

So if this self-replicating survival machine, in some unknown way, were to become conscious, what would we think its experience of consciousness would be like?

At the most basic level it becomes aware. It becomes aware of its surroundings – its environment. In addition, it becomes aware that it has an especially close relationship with a particular object of experience – its body. And when I say 'aware' I mean just that. It is aware of the existence of certain objects and how they are behaving in space and time, but nothing more. One would expect the mind to be but a *passive observer* of what is going on in the physical world – much in the same way as one might view a film on television. We can follow the story as it develops, but are unable to influence the events being depicted. Given that this survival machine's movements are entirely governed by the laws of nature, there appears to be no scope for the mind to intervene to alter the course of events. What will be, will be. One is able merely to look on and be aware of what in any case is inevitably going to happen.

But how does that tally with experience? Are we really nothing more than disinterested observers of what is going on?

Feelings

Touch a hot saucepan and one is hardly 'disinterested'! One experiences an unpleasant pain. Why do we feel pain? It is a warning. It is telling us to take evasive action; it is part of our survival strategy. The same goes for other feelings. The unpleasantness of hunger is a signal that the body needs food, thirst that it needs drink. Feeling cold is a sign that one needs to light a fire or put on more clothing. The pleasant feeling of becoming warm again tells us we have done the right thing. These are the standard explanations as to why we need to experience feelings, pleasant or otherwise. Feelings are a call for us to take actions.

All very reasonable. Except that it is not. At least, it is not according to the materialist point of view. As we have just been saying, according to this standpoint, we are nothing but machines operating slavishly according to the laws of nature. *There are no decisions to be made.* Yes, one needs to remove one's hand from the hot saucepan, or to find food or drink, or to find warmth. But – and it is a big 'but' – these actions are going to happen anyway. Through the evolutionary process, the machine is in a sense 'programmed' in its genes to perform these actions automatically. The future is determined. There are no decisions whatsoever to be made. In any case, the mind is, so we are assuming, no more than an epiphenomenon with no power to act in the world. It has simply, indeed helplessly, to watch what is in any case going to happen. Consequently, all feelings, pleasant and otherwise, are irrelevant; they serve no useful purpose. So why have them? They are surplus to requirements. What one expects to find in the mind is a purely disinterested awareness. But that, obviously, is not how it is.

So the existence of feelings is the first characteristic of consciousness that takes us by surprise – or, at least, it *ought* to take us by surprise. What else?

Free will

One of the most persistent problems in philosophy is that posed by free will. It is the common belief that the future is open, and that it is dependent upon what we choose to do out of a number of options available to us. However, in a famous experiment conducted by Benjamin Libet in 1983 it was revealed that when a subject was asked to choose a moment for moving his or her wrist, there was distinctive electrical activity in the brain about a third of a second before the conscious decision was made. This specific electrical activity is named the 'readiness potential'. Observation of this type of activity allowed the experimenter to anticipate when the so-called conscious decision was about to be made. This finding, naturally enough, was seized upon by materialists as proof that our 'decisions' were illusory; the brain had already determined what the outcome would be. Observation of the readiness potential allowed one to predict what the conscious 'decision' was going to be.

This, however, was not to be the interpretation that Libet himself put on his findings. He pointed out that one could well regard the electrical activity as corresponding to unconscious volitional processes, which only later were given conscious expression. Moreover, he pointed out that subjects know consciously that they are about to move the wrist about a fifth of a second before the action actually takes place. This gives them time to change their mind if they choose to do so. Indeed, some subjects spoke of deciding to move the wrist but at the last moment vetoing the action. In this way Libet seeks to preserve free will through the manner in which the conscious mind decides whether or not to go along with the promptings of the unconscious.

With the interpretation of that experiment being in doubt, we turn to a seemingly more potent and straightforward threat to free will, namely that posed by strict determinism. The idea that everything that happens in the physical world is determined by the laws of nature, and that from any given state of affairs, the laws dictate what the next state is going to be, seems, of course, to be completely at odds with everyday experience. As far as living our lives is concerned, the making of decisions affecting the future seems inescapable. Suppose for the sake of argument we agreed that the future is determined and there is nothing we can do about it. As a result, we decide that in future we shall make no further decisions and will simply go along with the flow letting nature take its normal course. The decision not to make decisions would, of course, itself be a decision. And deciding to persist with this attitude of not making decisions would be an ongoing sequence of making further conscious decisions not to act.

So how might we be able to wriggle out of the straitjacket of determinism and exercise free will? There is no consensus. One possibility is that when dealing with matter in the exceptionally complicated form of a human brain, new 'higher' laws might come into play. Were that to be the case, whatever happens in the brain cannot entirely be accounted for in terms of the laws with which we are familiar – those that are adequate for describing matter in its simpler forms. The coming into operation of the higher laws might then give rise to a mind that is indeed capable of making an impression on the brain. But that, of course, is a possibility expressly denied by the materialist claim that the mind is but an impotent epiphenomenon.

One way of loosening the strict causal chain of determinism is to call upon quantum theory. Without going into details, let me just say that at the subatomic level, a different kind of physics takes over. When dealing with the behaviour of tiny subatomic particles, one can no longer predict the future with absolute certainty. One can only assess the relative probabilities of a whole host of possible outcomes. This all goes under the name of 'Heisenberg's uncertainty principle', so named after the German physicist who first proposed it. It states that the more accurately one knows the position of one of these tiny particles, the less one can know about its velocity – how it is moving. And vice versa. The more one knows about how it moves, the less precisely one can fix its position. But in order to predict exactly what it is going to do next, one needs to know both its precise position and its precise velocity. According to the principle, this is an impossibility. Thus the future is subject to an element of chance; it is *not* strictly determined.

This all sounds very strange and counter-intuitive. It does not accord with everyday experience, where the future does appear to be predictable. (OK, when playing tennis, for example, the ball often does not go in the direction expected. But it would be a lame excuse to blame that on quantum uncertainty rather than a lack of skill on the part of the player!) The reason why the world appears predictable is that generally speaking in our normal everyday life we are dealing with objects on the macroscopic scale. What we are observing is the average behaviour of a vast ensemble of subatomic particles. Though the behaviour of its constituent particles is subject to quantum uncertainty, when dealing with the ensemble as a whole, the uncertainty involved is too small to be noticed. Hence the behaviour of the ensemble, to a very good approximation, appears to conform rigidly to the laws of nature – the law of conservation of energy, the law of conservation of momentum, and so on.

This quantum uncertainty has been seized upon by some defenders of free will. Quantum uncertainty does indeed break the chain of strict determinism and allows a degree of openness as regards the future. This in turn would seem to imply that if the process of 'decision-making' is taking place in the brain at the level where the behaviour of individual atoms comes into play, then various courses of action appear to open up.

But what are we substituting for strict determinism? Conscious decision-making in accordance with one's intentions? Nothing of the sort. We are calling upon chance – random chance. Recall how, when faced with a choice that has to be made, we sometimes resort to the toss of a coin. Is this the making of a conscious decision? No. Rather it is a case of opting out of making a conscious, deliberate decision. We are leaving it to chance instead. Quantum uncertainty is, therefore, no answer to why we feel we are decision-makers possessing free will.

An elaboration of this argument involving quantum uncertainty holds that some mental agency might act within the limits allowed by the uncertainty to produce the chosen outcome. Acting within those limits it does not violate any physical law. However that might be, this argument, like any other that depends on quantum uncertainty, has to face the objection that these uncertainties are exceedingly small – so small that it is difficult to believe that an event occurring at the atomic level could somehow be magnified so as to become an action at the macroscopic level of human action. This seems especially to be the case when one bears in mind that, on account of the brain being warm, its atoms and molecules are randomly jiggling about with what is known as thermal noise. Such movements are typically a thousand million times greater than the uncertainties due to quantum physics, and yet they do not interfere with the smooth operation of the brain at the macroscopic level.

Going back to the materialist position, there being no way of accommodating free will into such a world view, the response is to dismiss it as an illusion. When performing some action, whatever it might be, that action is governed by the laws of nature. It is the natural action that follows on inevitably from what was previously happening. And because it is *natural* for the body to be taking that action, the conscious mind – through its association with that body, and especially its intimately close link to the brain that initiated the action – is in agreement with that action taking place; it feels it 'owns' the action; it feels 'responsible' for it. This is called the *compatibilist* approach to the problem of free will. It essentially involves a redefinition of what one means by the term free will.

The illusory aspect of the common idea of free will resides in the thought that one could have acted differently. Yes indeed one could have acted differently if that is what one wanted to do at the time. But at that time one did not want to take that different course of action. That would have been a different version of oneself – one corresponding to a different state of the brain from the actual one. Instead one acted in a manner true to the actual state.

But that still leaves one with the question as to why such an illusion should arise. How did the mind come to acquire it? Why doesn't the mind simply, in a manner of speaking, sit back and contentedly let matters take their natural course? This seems especially odd when what one is dealing with is a self-replicating survival machine. In order to survive in a sometimes hostile environment it is important that the actions taken are appropriate to the actual circumstances in which one finds oneself. In general, the harbouring of illusions can be dangerous. They certainly are unlikely to be conducive to survival. Far better to have a realistic assessment of the situation. Why waste valuable time and effort contemplating various alternative courses of action when, according to the materialist, none of them can be taken?

The notion of free will becomes the second feature of consciousness that a materialist would not expect to find there.

Altruism

There can be no exaggerating just how harsh the evolutionary process can be. Premature death plays an integral part in it. It is essential that those unfortunate enough not to possess advantageous variations to their genetic material have to be eliminated; and, what is more, they must be eliminated before they have a chance of getting to the stage where they are able to mate and pass on their less well-endowed genes. There thus arises a strong element of competition. One would expect individuals to put their own interests first: they will be selfish; they will grab what food and shelter there is; they will compete to secure a suitable mate. This competitive spirit might well manifest itself as overt aggression. And all this is written in the genes.

We don't need to look into ourselves too deeply in order to find this self-centred trait. The urge to put one's own interests first is strong. Throughout our lives we are involved in competition with others. We encounter this as youngsters over our ranking in school tests and examinations. Later in life we compete over getting good jobs. There are likely to be many applicants for the same job, so we have to make the strongest case for ourselves. We might have to compete with other suitors over the person we wish to marry. We haggle with the sellers over the price of the house we wish to buy from them. It seems only sensible to get the best deal in all our commercial transactions.

On the larger scale we find that the firm we work for is liable to be in competition with other firms working in the same area. As a new shop opens in the high street, so another selling the same goods might have to fold. Banks steal a march on their rivals by poaching high-flying executives with salaries and bonuses that strike the ordinary person as obscene. One's country might find itself having to strike tough bargains with other countries over such things as fishing rights, oil exploration rights, the setting of tariffs to protect the interests of one's own industries, and so on. This is selfishness writ large.

Nor are we talking here merely of our openly selfish traits. Psychologists have drawn attention to the fact that in the social interactions of our ancestors, there could have been evolutionary advantage to oneself in being deceitful; that is to say, in cheating the other out of what was rightfully theirs. Thus one must expect to find in ourselves an inborn trait to be dishonest in our transactions. Indeed, the charge goes further than that. Those who are most successful at deceiving others are those who deceive themselves. People who mistakenly consider themselves to be altruistic and caring can be those most likely to exploit others. They are only dimly aware, if at all, of their true motives. This self-deception is brought about by a process known as repression. One is repressing the truth. And sure enough, there is plenty of evidence for this. At least it is obvious to us when we observe the behaviour of other people. The fact that it is less often seen as a feature of one's own behaviour only confirms the theory!

Our innate sense of being in competition with others can manifest itself in subtle ways. Take for instance gossip. We all love a good gossip – hearing about what other people are getting up to. But note that we are selective in what we talk about. We are not particularly interested in other people's sleep patterns, what food they prefer to eat or any such mundane matters. No, the topics of gossipy conversations tend in the main to concern births, deaths, who is going out with whom, divorce, scandals of any kind, money difficulties, wins on the lottery, promotion at work, redundancy, and so on. They all have some relevance to the idea of competition over matters such as social status and sexual activities. And in the main they concern people we know and come into contact with, so, theoretically at least, they could be our rivals.

We are not so interested in the activities of strangers we have never met and are not likely ever to encounter. With one exception: so-called celebrities. We have in mind those we see on television: film stars, footballers, politicians, royalty and others in the news. How come we take an interest in such people, even to the extent that some magazines are entirely devoted to celebrity gossip? The lives of such people seem to have no relevance to ours. An interesting suggestion is that it arises because we, in a sense, 'encounter' such personages in our home environment through the medium of television, radio and the newspapers we read over the breakfast table. Our Pleistocene ancestors had no such devices, so at some level of our unconscious the evolutionary imprints we have today inherited from them make no clear distinction between meeting people in the flesh and interacting with them virtually through these modern means. Indeed, these celebrities do not even have to be real people. How often has one found oneself concerned with the welfare and motives of some character in a soap opera to the extent where we hold conversations with others as to what the next episode might reveal. The fact that the character is entirely fictitious need be no bar to our having a gossip about them.

Gossip, as we have noted, is a somewhat more subtle manifestation of our competitive streak. At other times selfish competition can escalate and become overt aggression. One thinks. for instance, of burglary, rape, the infliction of grievous bodily harm, slavery, torture, football hooliganism, race riots, gang fights, to name but a few criminal acts. There are the atrocities carried out by jihadists. There was the Holocaust. There is the never-ending succession of wars throughout the world.

Of course, we ourselves would wish to dissociate ourselves from such violent acts of aggression. We like to think of ourselves as leading decent, peaceable lives. But the tendency to be aggressive is nevertheless there. It is simply that we sublimate it. A common channel through which it can be indulged is sport. Sport provides an alternative way of expressing rivalries between individuals, teams and nations. It is one of civilization's means for containing potentially dangerous tendencies so that they cause less harm. And not all sports go to the trouble of disguising the aggression. Here we are not just thinking of boxing and wrestling. What of the so-called 'professional fouls' meted out by footballers? Even that gentleman's sport of cricket, played with a hard ball, has fast bowlers hurling 90 mph bouncers at the batsman's head while indulging in fierce sledging.

All of this we find manifest in human behaviour and in human consciousness. And this is exactly what the evolutionary psychologist would expect to find there. Given that entities fashioned by harsh evolutionary pressures were to become conscious, this is what one would anticipate their minds to be like.

Thus far, so good. But matters are more complicated than that. There is a much more agreeable side to human consciousness than the picture we have until now painted. The human psyche is not exclusively about selfishness and aggression. How are we to account for that?

Take, for instance, the love of a mother for her children. There is no stronger bond. As a man myself, I can only conclude that this special relationship arises out of the way that the child was once part of the mother; the mother giving birth to the child. But whatever the reason, there is nothing a mother will not do for the child – to the extent of laying down her life for the child should that be necessary. All very laudable and unselfish.

But such altruistic behaviour is fully understandable in terms of evolutionary theory. Recall how what counts is not necessarily the survival of the individual but that of the genetic material. Mother and child to a great extent share the same genes. And as we saw earlier with the bird being attacked by the hawk, it might well be advantageous for the genes if the mother bird were instinctively to be driven to make a great display of herself as she leaves her young behind in the nest, thus drawing the attention of the predator towards herself and away from her young. By sacrificing herself, she increases their chances of surviving the attack, and thus being able subsequently to further pass on the genes to future generations. Hence we should not be surprised to find that a gene has developed in humans that encourages the mother to behave in this selfless manner. This type of altruism goes under the name *altruism on behalf of close kin.*

Indeed, evolutionary theory has been even more successful in accounting for seemingly altruistic behaviour. One thinks, for example, of one monkey grooming another – a helpful and praiseworthy act. Except there immediately comes to mind the saying, 'You scratch my back and I'll scratch yours.' And that's the key to understanding this and other patterns of behaviour where someone goes out of their way to help another who is not necessarily closely related. It is done on the understanding that those benefiting from these seemingly generous acts will, in due course, be returning the favour. The cost of performing the altruistic act is more than compensated for by the value to oneself of what one gets in return. What at first sight might appear to be a kindly, self-sacrificing act is more accurately to be seen as one of enlightened self-interest. Overall it is to one's own advantage to engage in such behaviour; it is not sacrificial at all. Such acts are known in biological circles as examples of *reciprocal altruism.*

It is easy to see how this trait could have become entrenched in the human psyche. Along with the other innate characteristics we find in the mind, it presumably became encoded during the Pleistocene epoch, when our ancestors were hunter-gatherers. Hunting for animals involves an element of luck. Some days you make a kill, others you do not. If you go through a long lean patch you can end up dangerously hungry. On the other hand, make a kill and you may have more than you can eat. So it clearly makes sense to enter into a reciprocal arrangement whereby the other helps you out on your bad days, on condition that you will return the favour on other occasions. The donation is being made at little or no cost to the giver because he has more than enough for his own needs. Whereas for the receiver it can literally be a matter of life or death.

So much for the hunting aspect which, by its very nature, is likely to be hit or miss. Gathering plants is a different matter. Either there will be an abundance of food available or, given a spell of inclement weather, there will be a shortage. This means either everyone living in that district will have enough to eat and will not need handouts, or everyone goes short and so is unable to help others even if they wished to. The development of the practice of reciprocal altruism would therefore appear to depend on there being a community where, at any particular time, certain individuals go short while others have an abundance of resources, this being due to continuously changing fortunes.

So far so good. There are clearly circumstances where there can be evolutionary advantage to be gained from this type of arrangement. However, there would seem to be even greater advantage were one to benefit from the favour but then renege on the obligation to reciprocate. Those inclined to adopt such a strategy are known as 'cheaters' or 'freeloaders'. Accordingly, because the cheaters have the advantage of only ever gaining from the arrangement, one would expect that eventually everyone would become cheaters – whereupon the whole idea of reciprocal altruism falls to the ground. That is why this form of altruism only works in situations where the individuals concerned are repeatedly meeting up with each other. Through such repeated interactions, each individual acquires a reputation as to how likely they are to reciprocate past favours. Based on observation of their past behaviour, those who come to be recognized as cheaters can in future be excluded from the arrangement. From then on, they are on their own, never again receiving favours.

This so-called 'altruism' is the key to understanding many aspects of human behaviour. It can, for example, explain why we care for the sick and elderly. At first sight it appears difficult to reconcile the existence of the medical profession with the idea of 'survival of the fittest'. If people are disabled or past their prime, why expend limited resources on trying to cure them and prolong their lives? From an evolutionary point of view they have served whatever purpose they had. So why help the 'unfit'? Reciprocal altruism provides a ready answer: there is likely to come a time when one might oneself fall ill or be injured and require medical attention. Most of us end up old, frail and in need of care and attention. In the long run, therefore, it is to our own advantage to support a system whereby vulnerable people are protected. This is not so much a case of two individuals coming to an agreement over mutually helping each other. It is somewhat more complicated than that. It is more the case of person A agreeing to look after B (who is not in a position to return the favour), on the understanding that when A in turn needs help, his or her earlier generous act towards B will be repaid by C – C acting on the assumption that he or she in turn will be repaid by D, and so on. It all comes to the same result in the end: one's altruism is reciprocated, even though the payback might not come from the particular individual who benefited from your act.

I began by perhaps giving the impression that evolution was all about conflict: one was continually engaged in fighting rivals. 'Nature, red in tooth and claw', as the poet Alfred Lord Tennyson put it. But now we see how this is not the whole story. It does not have to be a matter of always engaging in competition. Reciprocal altruism can to some extent offset the violent, selfish acts referred to earlier.

These acts generally come under the rule of law. There is, for example, the law against stealing. Certainly there is something in us that urges us selfishly to grab whatever we want or feel we need, regardless of who it might belong to. But society decrees that stealing is to be discouraged. This is for the obvious reason that it is in everyone's long-term interests if we can safely hang on to what we own. In effect,

it is a case of: 'You leave my stuff alone and I will leave yours alone.'
Reciprocal altruism.

Similarly, violent assaults and murder are forbidden by society. 'I
will refrain from harming and killing you, if you agree to refrain from
harming or killing me.'

All such agreements might go against the grain and be hard to
adhere to because of our inherent tendency towards pursuing our
own self-interest. For that reason, society demands punishment for
offenders who flout its rules.

Take another example: the question of promiscuity. It is only to
be expected that there is evolutionary advantage in the male spreading his seed (and hence genes) as widely as possible. One would also
expect promiscuity in women to some extent, through a desire to have
as many children as possible. But she has to look to the future care of
her offspring. She needs a mate who will stick by her and help care for
her young. This will incline her to be more choosy and more demanding of a mate who will be faithful to her.

The male will experience sexual jealousy as he does not want to
find himself wasting his energies and resources bringing up children fathered by some other male. A male lion, for instance, on
taking possession of a new female, will systematically bite to death
any offspring she has had by a former partner. Such behaviour has
a certain parallel in human behaviour. It is known that stepchildren
are at greater risk than normal of sexual abuse, ill-treatment and
emotional deprivation. Indeed, an important risk factor where child
homicide is concerned is the presence of a stepfather. Generally
speaking, the woman is inclined to be more forgiving of the sexual infidelity, but is more emotionally jealous. She asks, 'Do you
love me?' She is more concerned as to whether the liaison is likely
to break up her relationship and disrupt the support provided by
her male.

There is, therefore, an underlying tendency towards promiscuity.
However, this can be countered by the recognition of there being
mutual benefit if we all respect other people's partners. 'Keep your
hands off my spouse, and I'll keep my hands off yours.'

So what we find is that if one does stick to these strictures, then
in the long run it confers a measure of benefit on oneself (as well

upon the others). And that benefit can outweigh what one might have gained through giving in to the urge for instant gratification. It should, therefore, not surprise us if our genetic material has over time acquired DNA codes that lead to a tendency to behave in these seemingly altruistic ways.

It is sometimes said that science has nothing to say about morals. But that is not true. Some of those rules we have described are perfectly summed up in some of the Ten Commandments: thou shalt not kill; thou shalt not steal; thou shalt not commit adultery. Indeed, in the evolutionary struggle for survival it is important to know accurately the true nature of each situation we might find ourselves in; we need to know the truth. So there has developed a further rule that it is bad to tell lies. And that gives yet another of those Commandments: thou shalt not bear false witness.

All of this, of course, is music to the ears of materialists. For them it must be gratifying to learn that one can, in this manner, account for so much of what we find in the human mind – the mind of a survival machine that is sophisticated enough to recognize that there are circumstances where, rather than resorting to open selfishness and aggression, it is more prudent to adopt a strategy involving a measure of co-operation with others. This latter strategy has the added pay-off of being regarded by society as 'morally praiseworthy'.

But is that all there is to be said on the subject? Should we think of the word 'altruism' as always being in inverted commas, signifying that it is nothing more than a rather subtle form of self-interest?

To answer that I begin on a personal note: I have an adopted son. Why? Was it because my wife and I were unable to have children of our own? No. We already had two of our own. We wanted more and were perfectly capable of having them. But at that time there was considerable concern about the population explosion. We felt it wrong to add further to that global problem, so decided instead to give a home to a child who had no parents. Indeed, a mixed-race child. But why? Doesn't that go against the evolutionary strategy of proliferating one's own genes, rather than spending one's efforts bringing up a child who is not related genetically – one who furthermore was even partly of a different race? Yes. But there it is: that is how we felt about the world situation, and many people feel the same way. So how do

I emotionally feel about my adopted boy? Exactly as I feel about the children I biologically fathered. I truly feel he is as much my very own child as my other children.

The mystery deepens when I go on to consider how I feel about my three stepsons by a later marriage. Earlier I painted a rather grim picture of stepfathers. And undoubtedly it is true that children, on average, are at a somewhat greater risk from a stepfather than from their own father, this being in accordance with what might be expected on the basis of the stepfather's underlying animal nature. But that is not true of myself. Again I see no difference in my attitude towards my stepchildren than to my natural children. One of those stepchildren, Nick, was the lead guitarist in a well-known pop group called Big Audio Dynamite, formed by Mick Jones, the former singer from an earlier group, The Clash. One of Nick's golden discs is up on the wall of our lounge. I am as proud of that as I am of the achievements of my other children. And when sadly Nick died young of a heart attack, the grief was as intense as if he had been one of my own. And I am sure such sentiments are common among other stepfathers. What we feel simply does not resonate with what might be expected of us if evolutionary psychologists were right and we were nothing but evolved animals concerned solely with the welfare of our own genetic material.

But that's enough of me. How about you? Say you are walking along the street and you come across a homeless person huddled in a shop doorway. How do you feel? Compassion? Of course you do. You might be moved there and then to give the person some money. Alternatively, you might resolve to make a donation to Shelter – the charitable organization that helps the homeless, both the obvious ones we see in the street and those whose plight is made less public.

There is a disaster: people are starving to death in Ethiopia; or thousands are made homeless because of fighting in the Middle East; or many have lost their homes and relatives to a tsunami in the Philippines; or there is the devastation caused by an earthquake; and so on. Again, out of pity, one feels moved to do something about it – to respond when the appeals are launched. This results in our giving money that might otherwise have been spent on ourselves. Alternatively, someone might undertake to perform a demanding, and indeed occasionally unpleasant, sponsored task, the proceeds going to the charity.

But why? What does one expect to get out of such acts? One attempt to account for acts of 'genuine altruism' is to point out that often there is a pay-off: the approbation of others. Having an enviable reputation for being a generous giver can be a powerful incentive. One suspects many a prominent philanthropist, perhaps unconsciously, is motivated by a desire to gain the approval of society in this way. He or she likes to see his or her name listed on a plaque as being one of the benefactors, and especially as one of the main benefactors. Better still to have a building named after oneself.

But such an explanation of altruism, though doubtless true in many cases, also has its problems. The claim is that society approves of such acts. Society considers them to be good. But what does society consist of? It consists solely of survival machines like oneself. One is thus forced to ask how a collection of such survival machines comes collectively to consider unselfish philanthropy to be praiseworthy when the individuals that make up that society are themselves intrinsically selfish. After all, if one has a son who shows an inclination towards football hooliganism, it would be foolish to think that the cure for such undesirable behaviour would be for him to join a gang of like-minded football hooligans. Such an association can only lead to mutual reinforcement of shared attitudes. In similar vein, one must surely expect that someone with a tendency towards being selfish will hardly change course through being in the company of those who are similarly selfish. So why doesn't society dismiss genuine altruism as being just plain stupid?

In any case, what are we to make of the many – probably the majority – of cases where the giving is made anonymously? In such instances there is no approval from society because society does not know the identity of the giver. That is known only to the giver. Such private acts of generosity must surely count as genuine altruism.

Recent research work appears to cast some light on this problem. Subjects have been asked to perform mental tasks while their brain activity is being monitored using a functional magnetic imaging (fMRI) scanner. The subject is set the task of making a decision as to whether to receive a sum of money for oneself, or alternatively give money to an unknown stranger. When the amount one would receive exceeded that which would be given to the stranger, the majority (83 per cent) opted to take what was on offer. However, when the sum the other would receive exceeded that which one would get for oneself, no less than 50 per cent decided to be charitable and give the money away, even though it meant they themselves would receive nothing. So why the generosity?

The researchers found that, on examining the brain circuits when the subjects acted generously, this type of decision was accompanied by activity in the orbit frontal cortex – a part of the brain's reward circuitry. In other words, the subjects were rewarded with a pleasant sensation. On the other hand, when they acted in their own interests by taking the money and leaving the stranger with nothing, it was another part of the brain that was activated – the anterior insula, a brain area associated with disagreeable emotional states such as pain and disgust. Thus generous behaviour was rewarded whereas selfish behaviour was punished – a finding that I am sure most of us can corroborate from our own experiences of feeling 'good' when we are generous, and feeling 'bad' or 'guilty' when we do not respond to the needs of others. Thus the fMRI scan provides a neat explanation of what at first looked like puzzling behaviour.

Or does it? Where is the evolutionary advantage – the reciprocal benefit? There isn't any. Recall how I earlier said how reciprocal altruism only works in a closed community where there are repeated interactions between individuals so cheaters can be identified by their past actions and thus be excluded from the arrangement. With most acts of charity one never expects to meet the recipients of our giving. And even if we were in continual contact with them, their impoverished circumstances would mean they would not in any case be in a position to return the favour. So reciprocal altruism does not apply. Neither does altruism on behalf of close kin, because, of course, none of the people we are helping are closely related to us genetically. So how, under some supposed evolutionary pressures, did our brain come to acquire this quirky reward/punishment system – one that rewards actions that are not to one's own advantage either as an individual or as the preserver of our DNA?

The ultimate example of this kind of altruism is when one is prepared to go to the length of sacrificing one's very life for the other. As Jesus taught, and was later to demonstrate in his own life, 'No one has greater love than this, to lay down one's life for one's friends' (John 15.13). It was an example followed by many martyrs. Of course, these days the idea of committing suicide in a religious cause has taken on a different connotation. We are naturally appalled at the action of jihadist suicide bombers. But we must not confuse the issue. The latter commit suicide out of hatred and a desire to kill others. What we have in mind are those who sacrifice themselves out of love for the other. Jesus allowed himself to die with the intention of saving others.

In summary, we have seen how much of what we call altruistic behaviour can be satisfactorily accounted for in evolutionary theory as being nothing more than enlightened self-interest or, if close kin are involved, in terms of benefit to their shared genes. But following on from that, we have come across examples – and there are countless others we could have cited – where there is genuine giving with nothing in return, and where it is for the benefit of those not closely related. It is those kinds of acts that evolutionary psychology has difficulty explaining.

The moral sense

In dealing with the subject of altruism we began to broach the broader question of morality in general. So far I have no doubt given the impression that reciprocal altruism is a cold, calculating strategy. Before acting, the human survival machine weighs up the pros and cons of performing a certain action to see whether the expected return pay-off is going to be worth the effort of making the altruistic act. But that is not how it seems at the time. One does not refrain from stealing simply because it is against the law, or because one has consciously worked out that, overall, it is a cleverer tactic to belong to a society that has such a rule, or because one fears punishment if caught. We refrain from stealing because we think it is *wrong*.

Likewise, it is wrong to commit murder. Take the Holocaust. If it is true that one is nothing but a machine concerned primarily with promoting one's own interests, why be concerned about the fate of 6 million people of a different race, none of whom one knows personally?

Yet we are certainly concerned. The spectre of the Holocaust disgusts any right-thinking person. The Holocaust was pure evil.

Or take adultery. Yes, many, many people resort to having an affair if they feel their spouse no longer satisfies them sexually. As we have seen, one indeed expects there to be an underlying tendency towards promiscuity. But such acts are commonly accompanied by feelings of guilt. One knows in one's heart that adultery is wrong.

How does one feel about paedophilia? It is not for nothing that convicted paedophiles are separated in prison from their fellow inmates through fear for their safety. The abuse of innocent children is universally regarded with revulsion. It is pure evil.

As for war, there are certainly times when going to war seems the only viable option, the alternatives being even worse. How to define a 'just war'? Never easy. War might be the lesser of two evils, but it is nevertheless evil. And so one could go on citing further examples that we can all agree are instances of evil.

On the other hand, there are acts that are universally agreed to be good. We have spoken of acts of charity. These are often referred to as 'giving to good causes'. Why? Because we instinctively feel that such acts are intrinsically good; they are commendable. Unless one is extremely rude and inconsiderate it seems only reasonable to hold a door open to allow an elderly person to pass through, or to help lift a pram up some stairs if the mother is having difficulty, or to give way to an oncoming vehicle approaching from the opposite direction if some other parked vehicle is partly blocking the way. Most of us are kind to animals; we positively enjoy feeding ducks. We approve of those who, when out in the countryside, pick up litter left by others. All these acts, and many others too numerous to mention, are regarded as 'good'.

Thus we find that we can generally agree that certain acts are to be commended as good, whereas others are to be condemned as being evil. But where does this sense of right and wrong come from? In the physical description of the world – the world in which we survival machines operate – there is no call for distinguishing between actions in this way. Nature simply takes its course dispassionately. It was the Scottish philosopher David Hume who, in the eighteenth century, was first to point out that scientific facts were about what is and not about what ought to be. It is only in consciousness that we assign moral value to our actions. So it is only natural to ask how it might have originated.

The sense of beauty

We turn now to the appreciation of beauty and the pleasure it can give us. Can this be explained (away perhaps?) as an evolutionary adaptation to do with survival? Possibly to some extent, as we shall see. There are various forms of beauty.

Sexual beauty

Let us begin by considering a type of beauty that should prove easy to explain in terms of evolutionary adaptation: beauty in the opposite sex. So far we have concentrated on evolution by natural selection. This involved the finding of suitable food and shelter, together with the avoidance of predators. But there has also been another type of selection going on, and that is sexual selection. This concerns the finding of a suitable mate.

Take, for example, the question of the peacock's tail. It is hard to imagine anything more attention-grabbing and flamboyant. Does this not run completely counter to the conclusion to be drawn from natural selection that there is evolutionary advantage in being camouflaged so as to escape the notice of potential predators? Yes, it does run counter. The tails are heavy and require much effort to drag around. They make its owner more obvious and prone to predation. But there is a competing force at work here. Being able to display a great tail is effectively declaring to a peahen that its possessor is strong, fit and healthy. In other words, he is a desirable mate. And, of course, acquiring a mate is a cardinal requirement if one is to pass on one's genetic material to offspring. Hence we need to take into account sexual selection as well as natural selection.

We consider first the preferences of men. At first one might think that men would not have much in the way of preferences. If the overriding consideration is to reproduce, then surely a man would want to impregnate as many women as possible regardless of looks! It is not for nothing men are inclined to boast of their sexual exploits. They are also far more willing to pay for sex than women. How often do we hear the excuse, 'Ah well. Men are naturally promiscuous.'

While there is obviously some truth in this, it is by no means the whole story. Fathering babies is a necessary first step on the way to ensuring that one's genes will continue into the next generation. But this will come to nothing unless there is someone to care for the baby and bring it to adulthood. So one must also expect there to be in the male psyche a drive towards settling down in a long-term relationship with a suitable partner so as to be on hand to protect and nourish her and her child.

Assuming, of course, the woman's child is his own. As we have earlier noted, it is only to be expected that, as a general rule, he will not want to expend his time and resources bringing up a child he has not fathered – one who does not share his genes. Thus for men an important characteristic of a suitable mate is that she should be chaste – preferably a virgin.

Certain physical characteristics of the prospective mate may be suggestive of fertility and health. For example, younger women are more likely to be successful at having babies. One would, therefore, expect men to find youth attractive. However, there is no direct way of assessing a woman's age. Indeed, without a counting system, one's age would be unknown. Thus one finds throughout history that hunter-gatherers tend not to know their age – this is likely to have been the case with our distant ancestors. One must fall back on indirect signs such as a smooth unblemished skin, bright eyes, good teeth, full-bodied non-grey hair, vigorous behaviour and an alert mind. Furthermore, wide hips and large breasts are beneficial when it comes to giving birth to a child and to suckling it, so one would expect a man to take an especial interest in those parts of a potential mate's anatomy. It has been shown that men indicate a preference for women whose lower spine is strongly curved, thus giving rise to a behind that sticks out. It has been pointed out that such a spinal structure allows pregnant women to balance their weight over their hips better. This in turn implies that such women living in the Pleistocene epoch would be better able to carry on foraging during pregnancy without sustaining spinal injuries. Hence they would be more effective as mates.

With men exhibiting such preferences as regards what they are looking for in the opposite sex, it is not surprising that this encourages in women a sense of competition with each other over 'trying to stay young' with the help of cosmetics – to say nothing of plastic surgery. Also, in the Pleistocene epoch when evolutionary adaptations were taking place, life expectancy was probably shorter than it is now, so one's mate was in any case likely to be young.

As for women's views of men, they look for someone capable of providing for them and their children. In the Pleistocene epoch they also had to be strong enough to fight off rivals when necessary. Research shows that women look for someone who is tall, has a muscular V-shaped torso, narrow waist and broad shoulders. They prefer men who are 'high status'. Again this makes sense in terms of having a mate who is capable. Moreover, the woman would want this support in the long term and so will be looking for a mate who is likely to be able to resist his inclination to be promiscuous, and instead prove to be a faithful partner.

Thus it is indeed easy to see how evolutionary psychology has successfully come up with an explanation for these various preferences, many of them to do with physical characteristics.

But what are we to make of the current preference among men for models as thin as rakes? One might have thought that, when food was in short supply, our distant ancestors would have preferred fat women to thin ones on account of their carrying extra stores of energy in their fat. Not only that, such women could resist the cold better by being more insulated by the extra layers of fat. Indeed, there does seem to be some evidence that in societies where there are food shortages, there is a preference for stouter women. And, I suppose one should add, fatter women have the further advantage of being more cuddly than those who are all skin and bone. So why the current trend to prefer one's women to be slim?

Again, is it not odd that some women are regarded as attractive and others plain? Research shows that men prefer women shorter than themselves, having a symmetrical face with full lips, high forehead, broad face, small chin, small nose, short and narrow jaw, high cheekbones and wide-set eyes. Asian men favour women to have black hair, whereas non-Asians tend to go for blondes. But what has any of this to do with survival?

The same goes for women's preferences. It has been shown that there is a general tendency for them to be attracted to men who possess a high degree of facial symmetry, a broad forehead, prominent chin and brow, a chiselled jaw and defined cheekbones. But why should women find certain males, like George Clooney, attractive and others not? Why should the arrangement of their facial features be regarded as at all relevant to securing a suitable mate, for protecting one's young?

What we find is that we can account, in evolutionary terms, for why certain physical features of a potential mate might strike one as being attractive and desirable, but not all. We lack a full understanding of the nature of human beauty.

Art

How about the beauty we find in art? For a start one might question why there is any art at all. Why should our cave-dwelling ancestors have spent time drawing pictures on the walls of animals they hunted when perhaps it would have been better in terms of increased survival had they actually been out hunting? Why did they spend so much time fashioning axe heads into objects of exquisite smoothness and symmetry – resembling the sculptures of Jean Arp, which give so much pleasure today? The workmanship invested in them is often far beyond what was required for the utilitarian purpose of being an implement.

It has been suggested by some evolutionary psychologists that the popularity of certain landscape paintings might hark back to primitive times and have something to do with the need for our ancestors, living in the East African savannas, to find a suitable place to live. The ability quickly to recognize those features of the landscape indicative of a suitable habitat would clearly have had survival value and accordingly could have been selected for by the evolutionary process. It has been established, for instance, that people show a preference for scenes of nature to those of built environments. They favour built environments incorporating trees to those lacking such vegetation. It is thus concluded that paintings showing trees (which can provide shelter and places to hide from predators), rivers (an indication that there is drinking water), game-animals such as deer (good for hunting), a wide vista (so one can see potential predators a long way off and take avoiding action), and so on, are likely to be popular. The ability to recognize a suitable habitat in such an environment might not have any relevance today when it comes to choosing a home in a city; nevertheless, because that ability had survival value in the past, it might remain imprinted in the genes of modern humans.

This conclusion is backed up by a study in which children were asked to state a preference for one of several scenes: a desert, rain forest, savanna, mixed hardwoods and a coniferous forest. Why involve children? We are looking here for any inborn preference. With an adult there might have been some pleasant personal experiences of other environments, possibly masking what was innate. The savanna won out. It is argued that this could account for the popularity of landscape art such as that found on calendars displaying country scenes – a preference that surveys show is evident in all cultures worldwide.

That said, one surely needs to ask why we gain infinitely more pleasure from a landscape painting by Constable than we do from a landscape painting we are likely to find in a typical annual art show held in a village hall. The Constable and the amateur effort are depicting similar scenes. Thus the claim that appreciation of art is solely due to an inherited preference for scenes similar to those where our primitive ancestors wished to live might lead us to believe that both paintings ought to produce the same effect on the viewer. But this is not the case. The Constable possesses a quality that the other lacks. This missing element is sometimes referred to as 'the sublime'.

One might expect appreciation for the painting to depend on how realistic it was in its depiction of the scene – how closely it resembled what would actually be observed with one's eyes. In other words, how photographic it was. Indeed, some people do express a preference for painstaking art ('You can see every hair on that dog!'). There has been the suggestion that the popularity of such paintings has a sexual connotation. Much of sexual attraction is bound up with displays of one kind or another. Human males have various ways of showing off their prowess and gaining female attention. To be able to paint in such a realistic, 'photographic' manner undoubtedly requires a certain kind of skill. It is claimed that any display of talent and ability might owe its origins to some sexual source. But if that were to be true of this kind of artistic skill, wouldn't one expect women to appreciate art more than men? After all, it tends to be males (such as peacocks) who display to females, not the other way round. There is nothing, however, to suggest that men appreciate art less than women.

A further reason for doubting that evolutionary theory is able to give a comprehensive account of our love of landscape painting is provided by the overwhelming popularity of the impressionists like Monet and Renoir. Such artists completely eschew photographic realism, drawing instead on some other source of pleasure-giving beauty.

So much for paintings that might have a link to the requirements of life on the savanna. What about the pleasure to be gained from a painting of jagged snow-covered mountain ranges? One would not want to set up home in such a hostile environment. Certain evolutionary psychologists counter this by claiming that such paintings tap into a different, though related, primitive need of our ancestors. They point out that there was advantage to be gained from being high up where one had a good view of the surroundings and so could more easily judge where a good habitat might lie. What better viewpoint than the top of a mountain. No wonder, so the argument goes, most of the USA's national parks are based on spectacular, monumental scenery, and artists are moved to depict such scenes of grandeur.

Which is all very well, but one must surely take into consideration that if there are mountains, the surrounding terrain is likely also to be rocky and inhospitable. Not only that, but some of the monumental national parks are not based on mountains at all but on valleys. One thinks, for example, of the breathtaking beauty of Zion Narrows in Utah, where the visitor is enclosed at the bottom of a steep, winding valley. Not much of a view from that vantage point.

What of paintings not based on landscapes? One might think, for example, of a Turner painting of a violent storm at sea. Powerful, beautiful and deeply moving, but one would hardly wish to be caught up in such a storm.

How about the great paintings of artists such as Rembrandt? Where lies the appeal in a painting of, say, a haggard old woman? Is it the skill of the brush strokes and how the artist has rendered the wrinkles on the subject's face so realistically? Surely not. It has more to do with the way the artist, in some indefinable manner, has exposed the woman's inner character. Like the Constable landscape, it is endowed with the sublime.

And what of the more abstract forms of art, such as Rothko's broad swathes of colour, Jackson Pollock's drip paintings, and so on? These do not depend on conventional notions of technical skill as such. How often do we hear comments on such paintings along the lines of, 'My young son could do better than that!'? The popularity of such works seems to go against the notion that art is derived from what were courtship strategies displaying superior skill.

In an attempt to explain how the appreciation of abstract paintings arises, it has been suggested that the human mind has a preference for regularity and symmetry. In trying to understand the world, it is easier to grasp what is going on if one is confronted with repeated examples of the same features rather than chaotic randomness. This might have something to do with the popularity of, say, Damien Hirst's spot-paintings displaying a regular array of coloured spots, or Mondrian's use of only horizontal and vertical lines. But again, what are we to make of the many other successful abstract paintings that do not seem to exhibit any obvious regularity?

In summary, what we find from the study of art is that evolutionary psychology has had some success in providing an explanation of the pleasure to be gained from certain kinds of painting – the savanna-like paintings, those that display skill and those displaying regularity. But it does have difficulty in accounting for other types of painting and, in particular, why certain paintings are endowed with what we call the sublime.

Literature

How about poetry? There has been an attempt to account for the pleasure such words and phrases can bring as possibly resonating with some biologically based metre or rhythm. But surely there is more to the beauty of a poem than its tum-ti-tum rhythm. Much of the verse one is likely to find in a birthday card possesses rhythm, but that does not stop it being banal. In any case, much modern-day poetry dispenses with rhythm altogether, as well as rhyme.

Turning to other forms of literature, we find that storytelling appears to be a feature of all cultures. It is through the medium of story that one can explore alternative realities and see what others might do in the situations so described. As some evolutionary psychologists have suggested, one's interest in novels might have connections with survival in as much as fictional novels are exploring different strategies as to how one might behave in given situations.

Fair enough. But that does not account for why we gain additional pleasure from works by Shakespeare, Ibsen, Tolstoy, and so on, compared to those of cheap novelists of today. Indeed, the latter are generally writing about events in the modern world conducted by people like ourselves faced with similar problems. So on the face of it, one might expect the works of contemporary novelists to have more relevance to our daily lives than those of authors living long ago. Shakespeare often wrote about kings and noblemen – not the kind of people we are likely to have to deal with. Not only that, they speak in a style that is often not as it would be today. Yet it can be the beauty of that language that appeals to us more than the more realistic but mundane day-to-day language adopted by the modern novelist. So there is far more to our appreciation of literature than its just being a way of exploring alternative strategies vicariously.

Music

Any complete theory of the mind needs to explain, among other features, the important part played by music. A number of researchers have considered parallels between vocal expressions and music. It has been suggested that, in its primitive form, music may have originated from the manner in which one group of animals sends characteristic warning signals to other groups, identifying the boundaries of its particular territory and its intention to defend it. This could account for the different notes that make up music.

How about rhythm? When our ancestors switched to walking on two feet the act of walking produced a rhythmic sound that was more pronounced than that when moving on all fours. The sounds being made are more predictable and one finds that members of a group tend subconsciously to fall into step with one another. This for our ancestors had the advantage that there was silence in between the steps so one could keep one's ears open for one-off sounds from a different source that might indicate the presence of prey or predators.

Combining the production of different notes with the development of rhythm gives us music, so the theory goes. Moreover, this tendency to fall into step with a regular repeated sound accounts for why we might find our foot instinctively tapping out the beat of the music. And not only the foot, why not the rest of the body? Hence we have dance. What this does not explain, however, is why many pieces of music today do not rely on any recognizable rhythm – so-called mood music.

Next we note that music plays a part in the expression of emotion. Giving vent to our feelings vocally can be an important means of expressing anger to warn off potential enemies, or to indicate affection towards a potential mate, and so on. The idea has been put forward that making music vocally might have started out as an enhanced expression of the emotion, this then leading to what these days we would recognize as singing. The emotional impact could then have been reinforced still further by accompanying sounds, these in turn leading to the development of instruments made specifically for that purpose because of their voice-like character.

Music might have a certain amount of survival value through helping social cohesion. A group might express their togetherness through singing. Hence, each country has its national anthem; a football team's supporters are likely to adopt a song as their own. In addition, loud rhythmical singing, accompanied by drumming and war-dance movements, could be a means of intimidating a potential enemy. One thinks of the Maori war dance performed before a New Zealand rugby match.

A very different theory as to how music originated – one advocated by Darwin himself – is based on sexual selection. It holds that singing came about as a courtship display. It was a way of attracting a mate.

There is doubtless much to be commended in these various theories of how music might have originated. But is that all there is to be said on the subject? Not at all. That might be the way music began, but it does not address the question of why we respond to music in the manner we do. It is all very well saying that it conveys emotion. Conveying emotion, as we have just noted, can be functional. It was useful to our ancestors to give out signals as to whether one was feeling aggressive or loving towards another. But why, in addition, do we find some music sublimely beautiful? Why might one experience shivers down the spine and a tingling in the scalp at the climax of a

Bruckner symphony? How are we to explain the power of music to move us to tears? It does not account for why we like certain pieces and not others.

The making of music requires considerable skill. It has been proposed that it is the display of virtuosity from the musician that produces the response. But as we saw earlier, when this sort of argument was advanced in an attempt to explain why we are moved by great art, this idea would lead one to expect men – who are the ones who have to convince their potential mate of their prowess and hence their ability to be a good provider – would be better musicians than women, and women would appreciate music more than men. There is no evidence that this is the case.

Nature

As for the beauty of things that have nothing to do with human invention, we have only to observe nature. Consider, for example, how we react to the sight of a rose. I have a rose garden. Why? Would it not be more beneficial to grow vegetables instead? Vegetables can be eaten; they provide food necessary for survival. With a rose all one can do is look at it. The reason, of course, is that the rose is beautiful. It gives pleasure just to look at it. And not just a rose. We decorate our houses with many different kinds of flowers. We give bunches of flowers as a token of friendship. They give pleasure. But why?

Certain evolutionary psychologists have forwarded the following suggestion. In the Pleistocene epoch it was important to locate plants that could be gathered for food. Flowers by their often spectacular appearance attract attention. The observation of flowers in the distance might be indicative of there being good soil in that location. It would thus be worthwhile taking the trouble to go to that location in order to see whether, in addition to the inedible flowers, there might also be edible plants.

As I see it, the trouble with that suggestion is that the flowers are only capable of indicating that there might be edible plants close by; there is no certainty of this; one could be disappointed. Would not our ancestors have taken even greater pleasure in recognizing a plant that was actually edible? How come they did not find the sight of their equivalent of today's cabbage, spinach, lettuce, and so on, even more beautiful than that of useless flowers? Why when visiting hospital today do we not cheer up the patient by giving him or her a bunch of carrots?

Or take a rainbow. Each time I see a rainbow I am struck by its sheer beauty. Then there is the delight of waking up to find that it has snowed overnight and transformed one's world into a wonderland. And so one could go on indefinitely citing example after example of the things that cause us pleasure through their beauty. But why? Why do we feel this way?

Even Darwin himself was puzzled by this question. In *On the Origin of Species* he wrote:

> How the sense of beauty in its simplest form – that is the reception of a peculiar kind of pleasure from certain colours, forms, and sounds – was first developed in the mind of man and of the lower animals, is a very obscure object.

Mathematics and science

Scientists and mathematicians often speak of aspects of their work as being beautiful. This might seem strange to anyone who struggled with those subjects at school. But it is nevertheless the case that some scientific theories are regarded as such.

To a large extent it seems to have something to do with the idea of simplicity. For example, confronted with the bewildering number of different chemical compounds in the world, it is satisfying that such diversity can be accounted for by postulating that everything in nature can be described in terms of being built up from 92 naturally occurring elements. It then becomes even more satisfying to discover that these elements in their turn are built to the same basic pattern of a nucleus surrounded by electrons, the nuclei themselves being composed of just neutrons and protons. Thus is born order out of chaos.

In the same way it was once thought that electricity and magnetism were distinctly different phenomena. However, the Scottish physicist Clerk Maxwell was able to show that they were but different manifestations of the same electromagnetic force. Later came a further simplification with the recognition that this same force was also associated with certain forms of radioactivity, which until then had been attributed to a separate force called the weak nuclear force. The combined force was named the electroweak force. The hope is that this in turn will get joined to the strong nuclear force responsible for binding the neutrons and protons together in the nucleus. Theories such as these, capable of fusing together a whole range of seemingly disparate phenomena (rubber balloons sticking to one's clothes, magnets stuck to fridge doors, radioactivity and nuclear physics), together with the simple mathematical formulae in which they are often expressed, are valued for their having great explanatory power and are held by scientists to be 'beautiful'.

Indeed, many scientists claim that in their search for new insights into the workings of nature, they are sometimes guided by a sense of beauty. Some possible solutions to a problem are regarded as beautiful or elegant and therefore more likely to be correct, while others seem less attractive.

Can beauty of this kind be accounted for in terms of some evolutionary adaptation? Certainly it must have been important for our ancestors to be able to understand what was going on around them in order to avoid dangers and make use of opportunities offered. One can imagine them being rewarded with a sense of satisfaction at gaining some useful insight into nature's processes. So far so good. But a sense of *beauty*? That is more problematic. Why there should be an aesthetic pay-off in addition to the more prosaic sense of having achieved something useful could be another matter.

Beauty as a by-product?

We have found that we experience beauty in several different forms. We have pointed out that it is difficult to account for many instances of this sense in terms of its signifying survival value. An alternative suggestion is one referred to earlier when we pointed out that a particular developed trait does not of necessity have to possess survival value. Characteristics that do have survival value might sometimes spawn by-products. We saw how evolutionary psychologists speak of these as spandrels. For example, one might ask what the use of chewing gum might be, seeing that it provides no sustenance. It is simply a by-product of what really has survival value, in this case, eating. An often-cited example of the production of a by-product is that of cheesecake. We need to consume fat and sugar. Sometimes these essential ingredients are consumed in the form of cheesecake. But, of course, not everyone eats cheesecake. It is just one of several possible by-products that might arise. Accordingly it has been suggested that appreciating beauty might be such a by-product. However, it has to be pointed out that most civilizations do not have cheesecake; it is a quirky localized phenomenon. A sense of beauty, on the other hand, is a universal. How did this come about if it is merely a by-product that started out in some locality and possessed no special survival value to help it to spread?

The sense of awe

Closely associated with the sense of beauty is the sense of awe. This has been defined as an overwhelming feeling of reverence, admiration, fear, dread, wonder, and so on, produced by what is grand, sublime, extremely powerful or beautiful or the like.

In evolutionary terms, the awe evoked by something like a thunderstorm is easily accounted for. One fears being killed by a lightning strike. It can be a matter of survival. The same would be true if one were to be faced with a charging bull. All that bulk hurtling towards one would certainly provoke awe in the sense of fear. It is a signal to take avoiding action. Awe makes one feel small and insignificant, and so draws attention away from oneself and focuses it on the environment. Paying heightened attention to what is going on around oneself could clearly be advantageous, particularly if one's safety is at stake.

But what interests us are those instances where we are dealing with the other senses of awe – those induced in the absence of any danger to oneself. Why the feeling of awe when looking out over an ocean, or gazing at a mountain range, or looking up at a towering church spire?

Closer to home, as I write this I am in my study and can look out of the window and see the 250-year-old oak tree that dominates my garden. It is huge and craggy. A scar runs down its trunk where at some time in the past it was struck by lightning. I love it. It has a strange beauty of its own. It exudes a powerful presence. But why? We have already noted that we might have an affinity with certain trees that our ancestors could have used for climbing out of trouble. However, my tree has no reachable lower branches so it is blindingly obvious it is useless as a means of escaping some danger as it cannot be climbed (without a ladder). And yet I feel awestruck. Why aren't I indifferent to it?

One has the same sense of awe when one goes out on a cloudless night and gazes up at the stars. I find that this is especially so on nights when shooting stars are expected. But I cannot help asking myself why I feel that way. Yes, the cosmos is big. But so what? It is far off; it does not affect me in any way. It has no relevance for my survival. Why then don't I have a take-it-or-leave-it attitude towards it? How come I gain pleasure from contemplating the cosmos even on nights when it is bitterly cold being out in the open? As for those shooting stars – yes, I know they are nothing more than mere tiny grains of dirt coming from space and burning up in the atmosphere and are of no consequence whatsoever. But each year, come 12 and 13 August, I am guaranteed to be on the look-out for the Perseids meteor shower.

It has been conjectured that the sense of awe manifest in such situations originated with our hunter-gatherer ancestors in the deference shown by lower-status persons to the powerful leader of their group. A tendency to hold such a person in awe, coupled with a willingness to follow his lead, would have enhanced social cohesion and conferred evolutionary advantage over less organized groups. Deference towards persons exuding strength shows itself today, for example, in the way studies indicate that we prefer our political leaders to be tall. In 58 per cent of US presidential elections, the taller candidate has won. This has given rise to what is known among political pundits as the 'presidential height index'. But what has height to do with politics? Nothing. The explanation seems to lie with our hunter-gatherer ancestors preferring their tribal leader to be strong. Under the circumstances prevailing at that time, having a physically tough and resilient figure to lead the hunt over what was probably a wide and demanding terrain was an advantage.

It is argued that this sense of awe towards a powerful leader has in our own time become generalized and displaced on to other objects – objects exuding power of some kind. Whether this is so or not, of course, has to be a matter of speculation.

The sense of creativity

Another characteristic of humans is the desire to be creative. Many species show indications of being creative, but humans are in a league of their own in this regard. Just think of the way humans have transformed the world we live in. The computer revolution is but one aspect of the way life today would be completely unrecognizable to someone living 50 years ago. Being responsible for creating something new can give one enormous satisfaction. Creativity is a universal feature of all human cultures, so we must ask whether this points to its having some evolutionary origin.

Being creative is all about being innovative – coming up with something new, at least something new for the individual concerned. But at first sight the brain, as understood by evolutionary psychologists, does not seem particularly suited to this task. As we have seen, according to evolutionary psychology, the brain developed a whole range of individual circuits, together with their associated thinking processes, each adapted to meet some particular demand repeatedly presented by the environment. The brain has a modular structure, each element of which deals with a specific situation that our hunter-gatherer ancestors habitually encountered. So how could this array of separate mini-computers, each dedicated to performing a familiar and often repeated task, come up with something novel?

By way of answer it has been proposed that creativity might come about when several of these circuits become involved with each other. Though each individually is devoted to some routine task, if a number of them can be accessed at the same time and so can work together in a variety of combinations, that might give rise to novelty. That is one possibility. Another is that some evolutionary psychologists, though accepting the main hypothesis of the modular structure of brain circuits, have recently indicated that they do not entirely rule out some element of a wider-ranging super-computer ability, this having the flexibility to be creative.

But what interests us is not so much the mechanics of how creativity arises, as the pleasure and satisfaction it affords. In my own small way I find that on completing the writing of a book I experience this rewarding sense of achievement. As for my hobby, that is sculpture. My garden features nine large sculptures I have made and there are many smaller ones located in the house. I gain pleasure from having them around me and knowing that it is I who created them. In this I am sure I share the same feelings as Stone Age people fashioning symmetrical hand axes, probably the first aesthetic artefacts in the archaeological record. I am fortunate to possess one of these exquisite tools – or should I call them sculptures. It never ceases to amaze me how beautiful it is, and how much time and effort someone has invested in producing it.

Making sculptures today is but a minority interest. Painting as a pastime is much more popular. Who hasn't had a go at painting or drawing? From early childhood one has delighted in such activities – even if it is just painting by numbers – proudly showing off one's efforts to one's parents. I don't myself play any musical instrument; I have tried to learn but failed. But I do know that many gain great satisfaction from creating music.

In setting up home there is satisfaction to be gained in choosing furniture, curtains and carpets, deciding on a colour scheme, and so forth, all this in order to create a pleasing environment in which to live. Then, from the proliferation of cookery programmes on the television, it is clear that many find it rewarding to cook and prepare exotic culinary delights. Others go in for flower arranging or engage in crafts.

There is the creativity exercised by scientists and technologists in coming up with new ideas as to how the world works and how it might be manipulated for one's own ends. And, of course, there is the supreme example of being creative: the pride women can take in bearing and nurturing children.

These are but a few examples of the various ways in which one might attempt to satisfy this urge to be creative. But why do we show this tendency? What relevance does it have for the evolutionary imperative of surviving and reproducing?

Concerning the last two examples, there is no problem accounting for their usefulness in this regard. Bearing and nurturing children is clearly relevant. Engagement in scientific activities can likewise be useful as an indication of intelligence and a gift for problem-solving. But most of the examples cited appear to serve no obvious useful evolutionary purpose.

It has been suggested that the ability to produce beautiful works of art enhances one's sexual attraction. That being the case, one would expect creative people to have a better than average chance of marrying and having children who would inherit their parent's creative ability. In point of fact, the opposite appears to be the case. Though artists have something of a reputation for engaging in short-term relationships with the opposite sex, they are less inclined to marry, and have fewer children than the average. Not for nothing does one tend to think of the successful artist as a loner, starving in a messy garret, and the brilliant, but introverted scientist absorbed in a world of equations and mathematics.

So is it not strange that for most of us our creative activities serve no apparently useful purpose, and yet they reward us with feelings of pleasure and of having done something that was worthwhile?

The sense of purpose

Humans are endued with a sense of purpose. There are goals to be achieved. When one is young these might take the form of aiming to pass exams or to be a member of a winning football team. Later it can have more to do with seeking promotion and recognition at work. There is the insatiable urge to earn more and more money. Or there might be the aim of being a good mother bringing up children.

Such purposeful activities can easily be accounted for by evolutionary psychologists in terms of their being survival strategies. They are actions consistent with achieving benefit for oneself through competition with others. Either that or looking after one's children – those who share to a large extent the same genes.

But then there are other manifestations of purpose, the origins of which are more difficult to explain. For instance, there is the question as to whether life has an overarching purpose rather than being a fairly meaningless existence. Is there more to life than simply surviving for as long as one can?

By way of answer I imagine most people feel it is a good thing to try and make the world a better place. To this end many devote themselves to 'good causes' of various kinds. This might take the form of supporting charities to do with research into cancer, heart disease, multiple sclerosis and other life-threatening diseases. One might be concerned about animal welfare, the protection of the environment, missions to seamen, helping the aged or lifeboat provision. There are those who volunteer to act as unpaid guides to country houses or cathedrals out of a perceived need to preserve our heritage. There is the religious belief that the ultimate purpose of life is to do the will of God – more of that later. What I am saying is that there are many ways in which people see their lives as being invested with purpose and meaning regarding causes that seem to have little if anything to do with their own survival or that of their kin.

What is so strange about this is that the scientific description of the world has no place for the concept of purpose. It provides a materialistic account of what the world consists of – structures built out of atoms – and how these objects behave in a predictable fashion in strict accordance with the laws of nature. There is no need to invoke concepts such as purpose and intention at all. Matters blindly follow their inevitable course. There is no flexibility; there can be no other course of action.

As a scientist this is the approach I have to adopt. Nuclei fuse together in the Sun to form larger nuclei not because that is what they have decided to do in accordance with their chosen aim. It is not because they think the world would be a better place if they were to contribute to warming planet Earth by releasing some of their internal energy. It all happens strictly according to the dictates of the laws of physics.

But is that the last word on the subject? Is that the attitude I carry over into my ordinary daily life? Of course not. That approach, while being inescapable for the scientific investigation of the physical workings of nature, does not at all seem to apply to the business of living one's normal life beyond the laboratory. There one finds acceptance of the role of purpose is universal. The fact that we act in accordance with adopted aims in life is self-evident. So why is that?

The universal religious drive

The sense of purpose is nowhere more evident than in the context of religious belief. The belief that there is something more than this world is common to most if not all civilizations. The first known ritual burials go back 100,000 years, with more elaborate burials dating back 40,000 years. Ideas about God, or about gods and goddesses, or some other supernatural agents, can vary. But regardless of the exact nature of the belief system, it can have a profound effect on one's life, leading to adherence to certain rules of conduct, rituals, prayer and meditation.

Attempts to understand how we acquire and generate religious thoughts and practices come under the general heading of the 'cognitive science of religion'. This is a cross-disciplinary research field, drawing, for example, on psychology, anthropology, artificial intelligence, neuroscience, evolutionary biology, sociology, and so on. Our concern continues to lie specifically with the nature and structure of the mind at birth, so we shall concentrate on what evolutionary psychologists have to contribute to the subject.

Research shows that, whether or not one's parents are religious, agnostic or atheist, most young children start out with a natural tendency to believe in God or gods. The religious sense has great resilience, as witness the re-emergence of religion after decades of oppression in countries such as Russia and China. The recognition of an innate religious drive resonates with what was said in the previous section about how one senses that life has purpose.

There are two aspects to religion. First, there is the personal aspect, consisting of what one actually believes about God, together with what one does in private by way of prayer and devotional practice. Second, there is the social aspect – the manner in which like-minded religious people join together to engage in shared worship and other activities. The question arises as to whether evolutionary psychology can explain (away?) these features.

Let us begin with the latter of these features. The word 'religion' is thought to have its Latin root in *religare*, meaning 'to bind together'. We have already seen how there can, in certain situations, be advantages in acting together rather than in competition with each other. Belonging to a closely knit Christian, Jewish or Muslim community can ensure, for instance, that there are friends on hand to offer mutual help in time of sickness, bereavement and other difficulties. This being the case, there arises the question as to whether belief in God – whether a real God or an imaginary one – is to be regarded primarily as a commitment device for cementing together a social group, a convenient arrangement that confers advantage on the group's members.

This attempt to account for religion has been subject to argument and counter-argument. For example, one of the difficulties it faces is the price one has to pay for membership of such a community. The price can be considerable. In biblical times it could involve the sacrifice of precious livestock. There are the strictures of celibacy, repetitive (and to be honest sometimes boring) ritual, fasting, making pilgrimages, investment in costly objects and architecture and meeting other financial demands. Religious belief has admittedly the advantage of providing hope and solace to the suffering. But it is hard to see what survival value there is supposed to be in entertaining false hopes as to what the future might bring, if indeed they are false. If the supposed survival value of religious adherence is simply that of belonging to a mutual-help group, why not come clean that that is indeed the rationale for belonging to this group? Why add all the baggage that goes with religion? Why hasn't selection weeded out any such religious tendency in favour of group commitment devices that are less costly and onerous?

Countering this objection, some evolutionary psychologists point out that for mutual-help groups to work they must be policed so as to root out any who are tempted to cheat; that is to say those who join the group seeking to benefit from others but do not return the favour when it is their turn. Though there are benefits to be obtained by mutual co-operation, the benefits to oneself of cheating are likely to be even greater. Thus the detection and expulsion of those who cheat is important if the co-operating group is to survive. However, for most groups such policing is unlikely to be 100 per cent effective. Thus, so it is argued, there is evolutionary advantage if all members of the group share a belief in an all-knowing God who sees all misdemeanours and is capable of meting out punishment to wrongdoers. Those belonging to a group that accepts the existence of an imaginary super-policeman are more likely to stick together, thus enjoying the benefits of mutual co-operation. Groups not sharing that belief have to rely on fallible human policing.

But is that how religious people think of God – a moralistic super-policeman whose main function is to hand out punishments to those who don't toe the line? One hardly associates the old Greek gods with being particularly moral. The modern idea of God certainly regards him as moral, but rather than God handing out penalties for the infringement of moral laws, he is seen more as a god of love and forgiveness. In the view of Christians, far from punishing sinners he is believed to have sent his own son to suffer on our behalf.

A further problem with the idea of the super-policeman is that any group bound by such a device would still be prone to infiltration by cheaters. These are those who join the group, but who do not themselves really share the belief in an all-knowing God monitoring what is going on. As far as they are concerned the policing in such a group is a fiction, which, though compelling conformist behaviour for other members of the group, has no relevance for their own behaviour. Hence the attraction. Enough infiltrators of this sort would surely spell the end of groups bound by a shared illusory religious belief.

It has been suggested that it is precisely in order to counter this threat to the cohesion of the religious group that all the paraphernalia and self-sacrifice associated with religious practice is an integral feature of this type of group behaviour. It is there to act as a deterrent to non-believers joining. These costly religious devices are hard-to-fake signals that authenticate one's commitment to the moralistic supernatural agency that is supposed to be policing the running of the group.

The trouble with this suggestion, however, is that such a forbidding set of requirements for membership acts not only as a deterrent to atheistic would-be cheaters but also to genuine believers.

Atheists respond by arguing that the deterrent effect is not as great for believers as it is for non-believers. This is because believers hold that conforming to all these religious requirements will lead to rewards in the next life. This is an incentive the cheater does not share, so cheaters are more likely to be put off by the self-sacrificing demands of religious practice. This, in turn, assumes that religious believers are highly motivated by the prospects of supposed rewards in heaven. But is that the case? Fanatical jihadists might indeed go about their murderous suicidal activities in the belief that they will be rewarded in the next life with 72 virgins, but I suspect the incentive of 'jam tomorrow' plays a far less important role in the thinking of normal believers than atheists assume.

Yet another point to bear in mind is that evolutionary adaptations take a long time to be established within the genetic code. It is believed that little can have been established in *Homo sapiens* in the last 50,000 years or so (hence evolutionary psychologists' preoccupation with the extended Pleistocene epoch). But complex theistic belief systems and religious rituals must be counted, on the evolutionary timescale, very recent innovations. There does not seem to have been enough time for them to become part of our shared genome.

In any case, all this supposition that religion arises solely out of its usefulness as a device for binding communities together suffers from one further drawback. That is the fact that the majority of people who believe in God do not in any case belong to a worshipping community. In 2010, the European Commission conducted a poll of UK citizens which revealed that 37 per cent believed in God, a further 33 per cent believing in 'some sort of spirit or life force'. Only 25 per cent declared that they did not believe in 'any sort of spirit, God or life force'. This finding was backed up by a YouGov poll in 2011 that went on to show that only 9 per cent of the population attended a place of worship in a typical week, 63 per cent of the population having not attended a place of worship in the past year. Thus we have a situation where, of those members of the UK population who subscribe to a belief in there being a spiritual dimension to life, no more than one in seven actually belongs to any religious group. The majority that do not belong presumably hold the commonly expressed view that 'religion is a private matter between myself and God'. This in itself seems to indicate that if belief in God is nothing more than an artificial commitment device, then it is not very effective!

That at least is the situation in the UK, and in other countries in Europe that have become increasingly secular in nature. One thinks, for example, of the Scandinavian countries. However, it is not true of the USA, nor was it true in the UK in Victorian times. Here we have to recognize that there can be other forces at work promoting adherence to religious observance – social forces. As was pointed out in the Prologue, in those Victorian times it was the 'done thing' to be in church on a Sunday. Today things could not be more different. Absence from church has become the norm. It is in times such as these that one finds out what adhesive power a belief in God actually has, and, as we have seen, it is not as strong as some would have us think.

Which should not surprise us. There are so many other much better candidates for welding groups of people together. A sense of nationalism can lead to people joining in common cause to defend one's country in time of war. One cannot help but be aware that one belongs to a particular race with all its cultural inheritance. There are those who are activists working for a political party as a means of bringing about some desired policy if elected to government. One might follow a charismatic leader. One might join a trade union to bring about better work conditions and increased pay. One can join the gay rights movement, or try to save the planet, or support a football team, or become a freemason, and so on. An advantage these other commitment devices have over a belief in God is that with all of them it is agreed they are real. No one can doubt that there is a nation called Britain and a football club called Chelsea. But with an invisible, intangible God there is always room for doubting that he exists at all. Such lack of conviction, combined with the aforesaid demands of adhering to religious strictures, must surely act as a potent force tending to lead to the disintegration of any group held together solely on the basis of such a belief.

Yet another attempt to account for religion draws attention to the fact that, like many social institutions, religions tend to have hierarchical structures to them. From time immemorial there was doubtless advantage to be gained through recognizing those in one's community who had leadership qualities, together with those who were counted wise. Having recognized such gifted people, one follows their guidance. Accordingly, religions are structured so as to have leaders – bishops, priests, ministers, rabbis, and so on – and then there are those who defer to them – members of the congregation. Why should a person aspire to become a religious leader? In order, so it has been suggested, to gain prestige in the community and the perks that go with it. Why should people join a congregation? Because throughout evolutionary history it has been sensible to learn from those with a reputation for possessing useful knowledge. Religion, so it is claimed, is just another manifestation of this tendency to build social hierarchies.

There was a time when there was perhaps a grain of truth in this conjecture. There was no doubt that the vicar in his palatial vicarage and church was a leading figure in the life of the village, on a par with the lord of the manor. But that changed a long time ago. Today's television dramas more often than not portray the clergy as nothing more than bumbling figures of fun. And if today's clergy are unfortunate enough to live in an old-style rambling vicarage, they are unlikely to be able to afford to heat it. And yet people still put themselves forward for ordination to the priesthood and there are still congregations.

Any theory that religion is an adaptation fashioned by evolution by natural selection has to show how it enhances reproduction. For religion to spread as an adaptation, religious believers have to have more children than non-believers so eventually those carrying the religious gene will prevail. But does religion lead to more offspring? The signs are mixed. On the one hand, certain of its practices would appear to be orientated towards encouraging fertility. One thinks, for example, of attempts to ban contraception and abortion, and the prejudice shown against homosexuals (though these attitudes are changing). By way of contrast, there has always been the encourage-ment of chastity. In times past there were restrictions on when it was permissible to have intercourse with one's married partner. One was expected to refrain on Sundays, during Lent and three days before taking communion. Indeed, the practice of total celibacy has been widely commended. All of which hardly lends itself to expanding the influence of the social grouping through the abundant production of like-minded progeny.

But enough of religion as a social phenomenon. What of that other feature of religion: the personal aspect, the actual belief system itself? How did this set of beliefs about an invisible God come about?

It is at this point we set aside attempts to account for the existence of religion on the grounds of its possessing some survival value, and instead explore the possibility that belief in God is but a by-product – a side effect of other features that do help us to survive and reproduce. May I remind you that in the evolutionary psychologist's vocabulary the term by-product, or spandrel, refers to such matters as the ability to play football or ride a bike or skate or write or solve complicated mathematical problems. None of these arise as specific adaptations our hunter-gatherer ancestors formed in response to some challenge they faced. They are instead enabled by adaptations that were designed by natural selection for other functions. So it is that various attempts have been made to account for at least certain features of religion as by-products rather than adaptations.

For instance, there was advantage for our ancestors in being alert and sensitive to detecting the presence of other people and animals, some of whom might pose a threat. It has been proposed that this ability might have developed to the extent that it becomes what is known as a 'hyperactive agent detection device'. It is hyperactive in the sense that it leads one to believe in agents that are in fact not there, such as an invisible God or gods.

However, this suggestion regarding the origins of religious belief is open to the criticism that, should such a tendency exist, one would presumably mistakenly imagine further examples of what one is already familiar with, namely additional humans and animals. As one would be out to detect agents relevant to reproduction, these imagined agents would presumably be predatory animals, desirable mates, and so on. There seems no reason why it would lead one to the conclusion that there were imaginary unfamiliar superhuman gods, the existence of which had no corroboration in actuality. Those who do habitually believe they are being watched or stalked have in mind another person, not some mythical creature. And in our modern age of CCTV cameras, who does not get the feeling that, when out in a built-up area, one is continually being observed? But again, observed by another person.

An alternative suggestion as to how belief in God might have arisen as a by-product concerns the distinction between animate and inanimate objects. Suppose our hunter-gatherer ancestor sees ahead of him lying on the ground what looks like a stick. Is it actually a harmless stick or could it be a potentially dangerous snake? There would be survival advantage in having an innate ability to make the distinction between what, on the one hand, is living and could be a potential threat and, on the other, that which is not living. Moreover, there could be additional benefit in erring on the side of caution; that is to say, suspecting that certain things are living when in fact they might not be. It is this tendency to be overcautious that leads, so it is argued, to our imagining the existence of conscious life – spirits, perhaps – where in truth there is none.

A problem with this suggestion is that whereas it might make sense were this overcautious defence mechanism to generate imaginary malign and potentially dangerous spirits to be avoided, it is hard to account for why it has instead come up with an imaginary God who is the epitome of love and goodness and whose presence is to be embraced. In order to answer that kind of objection, an evolutionary psychologist trying to discount belief in God has to set aside this argument specifically concerned with defence for one based on the more general theory of mind (ToM).

ToM is the capacity each of us has from birth to accept that other people have mental experiences; one is not alone in this regard. As we have already noted, we have no direct experience of anyone's mind except our own. One might suppose therefore that in the absence of such first-hand evidence, a newborn baby would have to be taught that because the mind is associated with the brain, and other people have brains, it is reasonable to deduce, even without proof, that they might also have minds. Consequently, one might expect to be able to anticipate their behaviour in terms of their having intentions, feelings, and so on.

However, contrary to this expectation, the baby does not have to be taught this; it already assumes it to be the case. From the outset, the baby interacts with the mother as one intentional agent to another. Such an innate disposition presumably in the past conferred evolutionary advantage. It meant that the baby responded to the mother in an appropriate manner. And not only to the mother. Later in life it would have been useful to have been aware of the likely intentions of potential predators and prey. A natural openness to the possibility that others might have a mental capacity, and that their actions might be anticipated in terms of their having been driven by conscious motives, almost certainly arose as a valuable adaptation.

Useful though this ToM undoubtedly was, and still is, it can be inappropriately applied. It is argued that it can lead us into concluding that objects have purposeful minds when in fact they don't. For example, in one investigation children were asked why a rock was pointy. One response was that it adopted that shape in order that animals could scratch themselves on it when they got itchy; it was trying to be helpful. Another suggestion was that it was in order to stop animals sitting on it and crushing it. The assignment to inanimate objects of purposeful intentions is very common at an early age.

Adults too can show the same tendency to accord objects a mental capacity. Take for instance the plant called *Mimosa pudica*. It is a member of the pea family. On lightly touching its thin delicate leaves they instantly recoil and curl up. For all the world they look as though they have been hurt, or that they are embarrassed by the touch. Not surprisingly the plant's common names are 'sensitive plant', 'shy plant' and 'tickle me plant'.

Another inappropriate assignment of feelings and thoughts was provided by the stage play *War Horse*. This involved life-size puppets of horses, operated by puppeteers. Although the puppeteers were in full view of the audience this did not matter; one soon found one was no longer paying them any attention. Instead, one's concentration became exclusively fixed on the 'horse' – the realistic way it breathed more heavily after exertion, the way its ears pricked up when someone spoke, and so on. The audience was happy to enter a state of mind where the horses became real.

A further example of how the ToM can become overactive is in the anthropomorphic tendencies shown by owners to their pets. Pets have brains of varying capacities, so it seems reasonable to assign to them minds of some sort or other. But what sort? The tendency is unthinkingly to assume that they have the same kind of mental experiences as we humans would have in the given circumstances. But do they? It is hard to say, but one suspects that our ToM has become overactive in this area.

One further example: Susie. This is the name I gave to one of my first cars. This was in the days when cars were far less reliable than they are these days. She was continually breaking down. Often it was difficult to get the engine started, especially on cold winter mornings. She needed lots of attention, including a service every thousand miles. In short, she was temperamental. Of course, looking back I now realize how blatantly sexist I was being (weren't we men all like that in those days!). But at the time it just seemed so natural to conclude from such behaviour that this inanimate machine must be feminine. Again we see ToM was at work. And so it goes on. At this very instant I am writing this book on my computer. Who has not thought at some time or other that their computer has a mind of its own!

So how is this talk of ToM relevant to our discussion of religious belief? The claim by atheistic evolutionary psychologists is that an overactive ToM fully accounts for belief in gods or God.

Such a claim does, admittedly, have some merit. ToM certainly appears to have been at work with primitive, early ideas about god(s). For instance, the Sun was once thought to be a god. In various past cultures stone statues were thought to have god-like qualities. One recalls, for example, the biblical account of the Jews worshiping the Golden Calf. These days, of course, gods are no longer thought of as being so embodied.

Another manifestation of ToM at work in the past was the manner in which unpredictable happenings in nature – earthquakes, droughts, epidemics, and so on – were thought to be the intentional acts of God. Thunderstorms were regarded as manifestations of his wrath. Disasters were a punishment for sin. Good times were examples of his benevolence. Whatever could not be understood at the time in natural physical terms was to be assigned to an intentional act of God. This was the God of the gaps we talked about earlier. And as we have seen, the progressive plugging of the gaps by scientific endeavours has put paid to this line of reasoning. The explanation of such events in nature does not require any conscious agent.

And yet despite the jettisoning of these ancient ideas, belief in God has not disappeared. So is an overactive ToM still at work in today's modern versions of belief?

In this regard, note that we have now moved away from how we might casually talk about things, and the mindsets we might unthinkingly adopt. We have now entered the realm of what we actually *believe* – what on reflection we believe to be the actual case. Thus, yes, thanks to ToM we were happy to go along with the convention that the puppet horses were real; it was all part of enjoying a night out at the theatre. But did we actually *believe* them to be real? Of course not. Did we believe that the sensitive plant was embarrassed to be touched by a stranger? Did I really believe my car was being wantonly temperamental? When I finish writing for the day, do I really believe that the computer will go to sleep? When the weather forecaster speaks of the threat of possible thunderstorms, do I really believe the clouds are going to issue actual threats? In these and in so many other ways we are led by ToM to speak of the behaviour of objects in these terms. But that is all it is: talk. What one actually *believes* can be a very different matter entirely.

Nevertheless, the atheist will want to argue that belief in God is a different matter. Even though one might have stopped assigning a mental dimension to individual objects or actions, the overactive ToM might still lead to a more generalized belief that there is a Mind behind the totality of everything. That is the claim of some evolution-ary psychologists. But how is this supposed to come about? ToM does not lead us to believe atoms have minds, nor molecules, nor rocks, nor planets, nor stars, nor galaxies. So if, apart from living creatures (who have their own minds), the world is made up entirely of objects that have no minds, why should anyone conclude that the totality of these mindless objects will give rise to a Mind?

Regardless of that, however, suppose – just suppose for the sake of argument – that we grant that ToM has indeed led us to a belief in an all-pervasive God, would that automatically indicate that the God idea was an *illusion*? By no means. If there is a God, and he wanted us humans to get to know him and enter into a loving relationship with him – if indeed this was, in fact, the whole purpose behind our existence – would it not be strange if we came into the world with no idea that he even existed? Far from being a source of illusion, might not ToM be regarded instead as our God-given way of ensuring that we are alerted to the reality of his existence? That is certainly how I would interpret matters.

In fact, the same could be said of any other attempt to dismiss the truth claims of religion on the grounds that there might be an adaptive advantage in being religious. Suppose, for example, there was an adap-tive advantage in taking mathematics seriously. Those who were good at mathematics had a better chance of surviving to the point where they could pass on their superior mathematical skills to their young. I have no idea whether this is true or not, but it sounds reasonable. If one is good at maths then that is indicative of a rational mind and that could have been helpful in the evolutionary past when it came to finding food, shelter, impressing a potential mate and avoiding preda-tors. Would the fact that one was in this way able to explain how an ability to do mathematics became imbedded in the psyche mean that one now had explained away mathematics as no more that an adap-tive device – an illusion? Of course not. On the contrary, one might rather want to argue that the adaptive advantage of being mathemat-ically rational stemmed precisely from the fact that it resonated with the underlying rational structure of nature itself. In the same way, any adaptive advantage arising from religion could be interpreted as res-onating with an underlying religious dimension to reality.

One final point about the origin of the religious drive. Current research suggests that there might be a genetic basis for religiosity. The gene concerned is VMAT2. It is sometimes referred to as the God gene and it is supposed to predispose people to have spiritual and mystical experiences. It is a contentious hypothesis, but even if it were to be confirmed, would this undermine belief in God?

It is hard to see why. We have already noted that if evolution is to be regarded as God's way of making us, what could be more natural than his seeing to it that the evolutionary process had incorporated into it a DNA-induced propensity to be open to the possibility of other kinds of mind, including the Divine mind? After all, according to the religious perspective, the overall aim of life is that we should seek God and enter into a loving relationship with him.

How might God have built such a tendency into our DNA? We have described how the DNA molecule consists of a chain of smaller molecules, the order in which these smaller molecules are arranged constituting the various codes governing our physical characteristics and genetically influenced behaviour patterns. The overall form of the chain is that of a double helix. So are we to believe that God has somehow interfered with the sequence of smaller molecules in order to produce a code that manifests itself as the religious drive? Possibly. But I prefer to think that, with the religious outlook affecting every aspect of one's life, perhaps its code has more to do with the overall helical shape of the DNA. The God-directed instinct derives from the general structure of the DNA molecule rather than from a particular sequence of component parts it might have acquired by chance over the course of evolutionary history. That way God would not have had to interfere with the coding in a supernatural manner. The God instinct was inevitable. I hasten to say there is, of course, absolutely no proof that there is any truth in this suggestion; it is just a pure guess as to one way in which it might have come about. But I must say I rather like it!

The sense of the presence of God

Closely related to the religious drive, and perhaps most striking of all, is the sense that, even when there is no one around, one is not alone. A Gallup survey conducted in 1990 revealed that 54 per cent of those polled answered 'Yes' to the following question: 'Have you ever been aware of or influenced by, a presence or power – whether you call it God or not – which is different from your everyday self?' Religious believers, myself included, have a powerful feeling that Someone is always present. Moreover, this Someone knows one's very innermost thoughts.

Which is odd. Knowing that I have no way of directly reading the minds of other people, I would have thought that what goes on in my own mind was strictly private to myself. And yet there is this conviction that Someone has access to it; nothing is concealed. This is called the sense of the numinous.

What does it feel like? Certainly this Someone exudes a benign presence, indeed a loving presence. There is nothing threatening about it. And yet it evokes a profound sense of awe. One feels one is dealing with a Someone who is greater and more powerful than oneself. The feeling generated has much in common with what one might experience on entering a great religious building such as a cathedral, synagogue or mosque.

In prayer one senses that one is not talking to oneself. Not all the time, of course. There can be arid periods. This might be due to one not being in the right mood. Or it might be that, when faced with a choice of action and wanting guidance as to which one to take, and getting no response, one is in effect being led to understand that it does not really matter which course one takes. God is able to use either. But to set against these arid periods are those occasions where one has been wrestling with some problem for a long time and getting nowhere. Then, when deciding to pray about it, the answer comes immediately. I have myself on a number of occasions experienced examples of this. Sometimes the answer is so unexpected that one is left wondering where on Earth that came from.

The numinous manifests itself in other ways. For example, it might be a case of having hurt someone, and there is this persistent inner voice urging one to take steps to mend the relationship. Perhaps one has always profoundly disliked someone, and for good reason, but suddenly one realizes that they are not all bad. In distressing times when one is anxious and fearful, one might find comfort. When angry about someone or about the situation in which one finds oneself, a short prayer can bring calm and a more rational state of mind. On reflecting about the world one might be led to the recognition that, living in the affluent West, one is comparatively well off. One is then challenged to give generously to charities helping those in need at home and abroad. When one has done something wrong one feels admonished. This is commonly known as the voice of conscience. Not that the voice of conscience is to be regarded as the plain unequivocal voice of God. Persisting in actions contrary to the prompting of one's conscience has the effect of diminishing that voice, in some cases to the point where the person acts as though they have no conscience at all, no sense of right or wrong.

These then are some of the ways the numinous can be experienced. However, before proceeding further, let me make one point absolutely clear. I emphatically am not claiming that only religious believers have these kinds of experiences. Of course not. Although atheists do not benefit from the practice of prayer, they obviously are perfectly capable of experiencing a voice of conscience and acting upon it; they can feel the need to give to charity and to mend relations with others. They recognize that in order to give meaning to their lives they should devote themselves to a good cause. No, the difference between believers and atheists lies not so much in what they experience as to how they attribute these inner promptings. Where do they come from?

The religious believer attributes them to God; the atheist has to find some other way to account for them. The atheist dismisses belief in God as an illusion – an artefact thrown up by the evolutionary process. But how exactly has this counter-intuitive sense that one's mind is an open book to an invisible Someone arisen? If we are nothing more than a self-replicating survival machine, how has this illusion come about? As we have noted previously, falling prey to illusions regarding what is real and what is not cannot be good for survival. One needs to know what actually exists in order to be able to take appropriate action. No, this sense of the numinous is yet another feature of the mind that appears difficult to explain through the means of evolutionary psychology.

Religious experiences

As you won't need reminding, the declared aim of the exercise in which we are engaged is that of identifying those common, permanent mental features we all share and which are hard, if not impossible, to explain in terms of their having been fashioned in response to evolutionary pressures. However, it might be argued that I have already begun to stray somewhat from that objective. Not everyone has experiences of prayer. Not everyone shares the sense that their innermost thoughts are not actually private. Rather than being inborn features common to all human minds, these have the character of being intermittent interactions between the mind and something outside the mind.

Indeed, when certain individuals look inside themselves they find further examples of the mind seemingly being in contact with something beyond itself. For such people, these experiences provide further justification for a belief in God.

For instance, there are mystical experiences involving an ineffable, temporary feeling of oneness with nature or with God, accompanied by the elimination of self. There is the intense one-off 'born-again' conversion experience of certain Christians. There is the whole range of different types of religious experience investigated by Alister Hardy and his Religious Experience Research Unit at Manchester College in Oxford. These might involve feelings of trust, awe, joy, bliss or ecstasy. Others engage the senses: seeing lights, hearing voices or feeling that one is being touched.

For those individuals who have first-hand experience of such phenomena it is likely that these features of one's inner life are the ones most potent in shaping one's spiritual beliefs. Indeed, when theologians declare that the search for God begins within oneself, it might well be that, for some at least, what they have in mind are these types of experience. But that is not the approach being adopted in this book. We are not concerned with the transient experiences of a limited number of individuals. Our approach does not depend on the reader having had these experiences.

Of course, it could be argued that even if not everyone has these experiences, that does not rule out the possibility that we all share from birth a capacity, or tendency, to have them. Indeed, research shows that such experiences are widespread, transcending cultures and belief systems. What might be lacking for any given individual might be an adequate trigger to manifest this underlying capacity. It is known, for example, that even an avowed atheist might in conditions of extreme danger find themselves involuntarily issuing a prayer. But if an individual has had no religious experience, and never feels the need to pray, then one cannot blame him or her for doubting that they do have such an underlying tendency.

No. We shall continue to concentrate on those features we can all agree are indispensable to the working of all human minds, namely the possession of feelings, the need to make decisions, the appreciation of beauty, the experience of awe, the moral sense, being creative and purposeful – those features of the mind that are hard if not impossible to account for in terms of evolutionary psychology or, indeed, other approaches to the psychology of the mind.

The mind: other approaches

Evolutionary psychology is a fairly new scientific discipline. But, of course, attempts to understand the mind date from long ago. As far back as the nineteenth century the view began to form that the thoughts of which we are aware at any time make up only part of the contents of the mind. In order to explain certain aspects of conscious experience, it became helpful to postulate an additional part of the mind: the unconscious. This was held to be capable of influencing the conscious mind through the production of dreams and hallucinations, as well as accounting for involuntary acts, such as slips of the tongue and other faulty actions.

The unconscious is a postulate: there is no incontrovertible, deductive proof of its existence. We have no way of entering and examining the unconscious directly. As soon as one thinks about a supposed aspect of the unconscious, the very act of thinking about it means that it has now been absorbed into consciousness. The existence of the unconscious can only be inferred through the way it appears to have an impact upon consciousness from outside, so to speak. For example, one has no conscious control over the contents of one's dreams. The explanatory power of the hypothesis is so great that the existence of the unconscious is universally accepted.

In order to progress further we need to know more about the unconscious, particularly as regards what it is likely to contain. The study of the mind from the point of view of an evolutionary psychologist has proved a fruitful approach to understanding how our conscious thoughts and attitudes are moulded by an underlying architecture of the mind. But other strategies have also proved fruitful in the past. To illustrate this we look at the work of two prominent psychologists: Sigmund Freud and Carl Jung.

Sigmund Freud

Some insight into the workings of the mind is afforded by the practice of psychoanalysis as pioneered by Sigmund Freud. He held that an understanding of the unconscious begins with the recognition of two kinds of content: the *id* and the *superego*. The id is something we possess from birth. It is associated with instinctual drives towards infantile gratification. These are to be thought of as essentially sexual. The superego, on the other hand, is derived from the environment. It consists of the attitudes of mind absorbed from other people – the standards of behaviour expected by society, especially those originating from one's parents. These beliefs are acquired in early childhood by an unconscious process that leaves one unaware of their origin. A tension is then set up between the centre of one's consciousness, called the *ego*, and the value system so assimilated. From this is derived one's 'conscience'. Because the behaviour dictated by this set of beliefs often runs counter to that which would arise from self-gratification, the id and the superego come into conflict. This results in those thoughts regarded as shameful, painful, disagreeable or alarming being repressed into the unconscious. Although repressed, these thoughts can, nevertheless, affect behaviour. In neurotic personalities these can have a debilitating effect, giving rise to unreasonable fears and compulsive actions. The aim of psychoanalysis is to bring these unconscious thoughts into the conscious mind so that they can be dealt with rationally. All of us have repressed thoughts, not just those accounted neurotic. The difference is that most of us are able to channel the drive stemming from such thoughts into some socially acceptable activity.

What did Freud specifically have to say about the unconscious in relation to religious experience? Though at times he could be somewhat ambivalent in his attitude to religion, he generally spoke as an atheist. It is important to note, however, that his atheism did not come about as a result of the development of psychoanalysis. Though certain of his followers claimed that it was psychoanalysis that destroyed the credibility of religion, Freud himself consistently denied this. He had formed an atheistic outlook from early childhood. His view of religion, therefore, was something *added* to his psychological findings and theories, rather than something drawn out of them.

Freud took over, and further developed, an idea originated by Ludwig Feuerbach, 150 years ago. This held that God was nothing more than an idealized psychologically projected image of a human being. It is human qualities of personhood, including love, sense of justice, wisdom, and so on that are externalized by the mind and become an object of worship. Why should only the good aspects of humankind be so projected, rather than an image of its totality, warts and all? Wish fulfilment. That is to say, the gratification in fantasy of that which is denied in reality. A particularly important example of wish fulfilment, so it is claimed, concerns our natural desire to feel protected. In childhood, a sense of security is generally provided by the presence of one's earthly father. On reaching adulthood, however, this protection is lost. At this point, wish fulfilment takes over. It gives rise to a belief in God, who can assume the vacated role of the protective father figure. Accordingly, belief in God is to be interpreted as nothing more than a prolongation of an infantile dependence on an earthly father – an avoidance of the need to face up to the harsher realities of life. The loss of the earthly father figure – either through death or through the recognition in later life of his inadequacies, at least in respect of his being able to continue indefinitely providing protection – is something that affects us all. For this reason it is not surprising that the community of religious believers is able to reach a consensus over the nature of God as a benign father figure. Having given rise to a belief in God, wish fulfilment goes on to endow him with further desirable attributes. We want his protection to be complete, so we regard him as omnipotent. We desire justice in an unjust world, so he becomes a God of justice. We wish to be loved, so God is a Heavenly Father who loves us. We wish to go on living indefinitely, so we believe in a life hereafter.

How are we to assess such a theory of religious experience? As a preliminary, it needs to be remarked that the general view of the unconscious so far presented – that it constitutes, in effect, a dustbin for unwanted thoughts – straight away casts some doubts on its being the main source of religious experience. It is hard to account for how such a morass could give rise to the sense of wonder, awe, beauty and nobility associated with the sense of the numinous. Any discussion of the origin of religious experience must surely pay due attention to the quality of the experience, and whether or not it correlates with the nature of that which is supposedly giving rise to it. Second, it has to be noted that although some people do admittedly develop unhealthy religious obsessions – perhaps being overwhelmed by an exaggerated sense of guilt – this is not common. It is far more usual to find religion regarded as life-enhancing and fulfilling, the very antithesis of a debilitating mental disorder. To be taken into account, therefore, is not only the quality of the experience, but the fruits to which it gives rise.

Next, we note that all of Freud's pronouncements on religion were founded on assertion alone; there was, and is, no proof for them. Even if one does accept that wish fulfilment is at work to some extent, this does not of itself, of course, determine one way or the other whether that which is wished for actually exists or not.

The notion that religion is grounded in wish fulfilment does not give due weight to the extent to which religious believers are *challenged* by their faith, rather than comforted by it. The very phrase 'being comforted', when used in a religious context, more often means 'being strengthened' (to carry out some task) than being merely made to feel reassured. In the lives of many great religious figures – Moses, Jonah, Jeremiah and others – we find them being forced into taking courses of action that were *against* their own wishes. Jesus himself, on the night that he was betrayed, asked that the cup of suffering be removed. So much of religious belief is to do with self-denial, not self-gratification. Again and again one confesses that one has wishes that are immoral. One asks for God's help, not that such wishes be satisfied, but that they be resisted. Of course, it can be countered that the superego has gained the upper hand. Fair enough. A victory for the superego is, in the language of the religious believer, a victory for God. But there is no denying that each win for the superego can be a wish not fulfilled.

Another reason for believing wish fulfilment to be less important for religion than Freud imagined comes from studying the prevalence of religion according to social status. Wish fulfilment, as already mentioned, is the gratification in fantasy of what is denied in reality. This being so, it ought mostly to be in evidence among working-class people – those deprived of both worldly goods and social esteem. Yet in those countries where statistics are most reliable, the UK and USA, working-class people are less interested in religion – the opposite of what is expected according to the theory of wish fulfilment. Rather than turn to a fantasy belief in God, they look to whatever economic system they think is likely to afford the greater material benefit, be it socialism, communism or capitalism – 'religions' in the wider sense.

Perhaps the aspect of religious belief that appears, from the outside at least, to be the most open to the accusation of wish fulfilment is the idea of an afterlife – the belief that the future offers some form of compensation for the injustices of this present life. But as we have already noted, only those who are themselves believers can appreciate just how little in fact the notion of rewards in an afterlife is the motivating force. Most of them see the religious way of life as the means of achieving one's potential and fulfilment in *this* life, and this holds good regardless of whatever the consequences might be for a future existence. Again, there are many believers who, if pressed, admit to having little or no belief in an afterlife – despite what they might recite in the Creed each week. Even in the Middle Ages, when thoughts of the afterlife were given more prominence in preaching and teaching than they are now, it was not so much the forthcoming joy of heaven that was held in prospect as the terrible consequences of being sent to hell.

This is not to deny that most of us from time to time indulge in wish fulfilment. We fantasize over our supposed abilities and importance. This being so, it would be unreasonable to imagine religious beliefs to be immune from this insidious tendency. Indeed, one has only to look back over the course of history, or at one's own personal life, to see instances of the image of God being manipulated to make it conform to some desired end – the justification of courses of action that perhaps only later come to be seen as self-interested and out of keeping with a more consistent view of the nature of God.

But while fully accepting the need for the religious believer to be on his or her guard over wish fulfilment, it is only fair to point out that the atheist is equally open to the same influence. Can it not be argued that atheism might sometimes arise out of a desire to consider oneself independent and self-sufficient, master of one's own destiny? Could one not find in certain atheists a wish to evade the uncomfortable, self-denying, demands of religious commitment? If even the most devout believers can sometimes find themselves daunted by the magnitude of the tasks laid upon them by the sense of doing one's religious duty, to say nothing of the cost imposed in terms of time, effort and money, it would be hardly surprising if some people, through the process of wish fulfilment, manage to convince themselves that they have no such responsibilities. In this way one sees that the argument against religious belief on the grounds that it is merely a manifestation of wish fulfilment is easily turned on its head.

The idea of a Heavenly Father being nothing more than a projection of childish fantasies concerning one's own earthly father is likewise a claim that can be turned around. This was pointed out by Jung, who held that Freud's concept of the superego could be regarded as just another name for the repressed and rejected God experience. In other words, it is an introjected God – 'a furtive attempt to smuggle in the time-honoured image of Jehovah in the dress of psychological theory'. Accordingly, God is not conceived of as a substitute for the physical father; rather the physical father is a child's first substitute for God. Whereas Freud saw religion as a symptom of psychological illness, Jung saw the *absence* of religious experience as the root of adult psychological illness.

One further point should be made about Freud's suggestion that God is a projection of one's earthly father: it goes no way towards explaining Eastern religions. Unlike Judaism, Christianity and Islam, these do *not* draw on the father figure image. Indeed, Western religions are little more than caricatured if they are represented as a belief in a crude, larger-than-life father figure. The projected father-figure hypothesis, therefore, at best addresses only naive versions of Western religions and cannot in any way be regarded as a comprehensive explanation of worldwide religion based on fully developed theological consideration of the nature of God.

In summary, we conclude that, no matter how justly pre-eminent Freud was in other areas of psychology, when it came to religion his pronouncements were at best arbitrary. He tended to attack particularly unsophisticated forms of religious belief, and even that was done unconvincingly. Not surprisingly, his chief works on religious subjects – *Totem and Taboo*, *The Future of an Illusion* and *Moses and Monotheism* – are today among the most neglected of his books among serious psychologists. The arguments they contain are rejected with remarkable unanimity by most specialists in the subjects around which they are based.

Before leaving the subject of Freud, however, it is only fair to point out that the study of his work does have a positive side in helping us understand better the nature of our religious beliefs. Rightly we reject his main thesis regarding the origin of religious experience. But it would be foolish to think that he had nothing of value to offer. For those of us who subscribe to a religion that draws on the Heavenly Father metaphor, we would do well to be alive to the possibility of that image being too heavily overlain with inappropriate connotations deriving from our view of the role of an earthly father. Surveys have shown that those who have had a strict upbringing tend to regard God as more severe than those who have been brought up by parents who were more easy-going. With the wholesale changes that have taken place in society in recent times, especially regarding attitudes towards parents and those in positions of authority in general, we could find ourselves unconsciously adopting a changed attitude towards God. This might or might not be a good thing, but at least we ought to be aware that it is happening.

Carl Jung

Someone with a more profound appreciation of religion than Freud was Carl Jung. On the basis of his own deeply felt first-hand experience of religion, Jung sought to incorporate religious insights into his study of the unconscious mind.

His work begins with the recognition that the unconscious contains much more than had hitherto been suspected. In particular, an aspect of the unconscious that we all share: that which is innate and does not depend upon the circumstances of the individual's own life. His studies led him to the conclusion that in a wide variety of situations we all tend to think and act in similar ways. This he discovered long before today's evolutionary psychologists came to adopt the same idea as the basis of their discipline. These common traits arise not because we have been taught to react so. Rather, from birth, these predispositions lie dormant deep within the unconscious awaiting a suitable occasion to give expression to themselves. These patterns of potential thought and behaviour constitute what he called the *collective unconscious*. It is to be seen as a pre-existing framework into which the events of the individual's life history are received. One's experiences are moulded by the structure of that framework, as well as by whatever previous experiences the individual has had. It is something like a jelly mould. The mould starts out empty; it has no contents. But once it receives the poured jelly mix it comes into play, shaping the eventual jelly. The collective unconscious consists of various component features. These Jung called *archetypes*. The term derives from the Greek words *arche*, meaning 'beginning', and *typos*, meaning 'imprint'.

Thus, according to Jung, an individual's unconscious is characterized by two aspects: that which derives from the individual's past experiences and that which is shaped by the collective unconscious. The first is specific to the individual, the second is innate and common to us all.

The notion of a collective unconscious fits in well with what we have learned from evolutionary theory. There we discovered that in our inherited DNA there are codes to do with genetically influenced behaviour patterns, these being adaptations or by-products of those adaptations. As a first approximation one can say that Jung's idea of a collective unconscious bears an uncanny similarity to the kind of conclusions drawn by today's evolutionary psychologist.

He arrived at this insight, however, by a very different route. Jung began his investigation by carefully considering his own dreams and those of his patients. He paid particular attention to those aspects that did not seem to have any direct connection with the actual experiences of the one reporting the dream. He also analysed the fantasies and delusions of the insane. He studied comparative religion and especially mythological stories, seeking out recurring themes. These he found to be common to many disparate cultures all over the world, and throughout human history. There was a universal quality about them.

The archetypes represented certain regularities or consistently recurring types of situation and figures. How many archetypes are there? It is hard to say. One expects as many archetypes as there are typical repeated circumstances conferring survival advantage on those with the appropriate genetic make-up. Jung was able to delineate many of them. He found archetypes associated with psychological dispositions towards various figures: mother, father, family, hero, wise old man, and so on, as well as those associated with situations arising out of one's relationship to such figures.

As an example, let us take the mother archetype. A baby on being presented to the breast for the first time instinctively knows that it has to suck. It does not need to be taught this because this knowledge is already encoded into its genetic make-up. It is behaviour that arose in the course of evolution through natural selection in the far distant past when mammals first put in an appearance. Since that time, any mammalian offspring that lacked the appropriate gene failed to get sustenance and so did not survive to the point where they could themselves mate and pass on the gene lacking in this characteristic. That is how the situation is described in terms of evolutionary biology. In the mental domain, the corresponding predisposition the baby has towards the mother – the thought forms that give rise to the sucking behaviour – derive from the mother archetype. Not that this is all there is to the mother archetype. Breastfeeding is but one small, rather superficial aspect of an intricate and far-reaching set of thought patterns controlled by this archetype. The archetype orientates us from birth to expect a mother who will nurture, protect, care and love, and, it should be added, a mother who might abandon, withhold, deprive, destroy and hate. In all kinds of ways, this archetype predisposes us as to how we relate to our mother and to mother figures; it can even affect the way we relate to women in general.

According to Jung, one of our natural tendencies is to possess a religious drive. He held that one ignored this at one's peril. If it did not find its outlet as a belief in God then it would be diverted into other channels. He declared that 'whenever the Spirit of God is excluded from human consideration, an unconscious substitute takes its place'. It might, for instance, manifest itself in a devotion to some other cause, such as campaigning for women's rights, a concern for the environment, an avid devotion to a football team, joining with others to oppose the building of nuclear power stations, fighting for one's country in time of war, and so on.

One can even see the same religious drive at work in the protests *against* religion of people like Richard Dawkins. In a sense, atheism is his religion. In one of his attacks on religion he likens it to a virus. The mistaken notion of religion, he claims, is insidiously passed on through what parents tell their children when their developing minds are particularly receptive. In this manner, this dangerous and unwelcome idea is spread throughout the world, polluting the natural state of the mind, much like an unwanted virus invades the human body. This alien idea has to be eliminated. Such is his claim. The flaw in the argument is that the natural state of the mind is to be religious. What is new and spreading is atheism. If there is a mental virus of some kind it is more likely to be atheism than religion.

Are the images thrown up into consciousness by the archetypes to be regarded as nothing more than the psychological correlates of genetically influenced behaviour? If so, it should be possible to see how each of the thought forms controlled by the archetypes in the mental domain leads to behaviour in the physical domain that is conducive to the survival of the individual or its close kin. We have already noted that to a large extent we do consciously act in such ways, engaging in selfishness, competitiveness and, if necessary, aggression. Sometimes we co-operate with others when the favour is to be reciprocated. But having said that, it has to be added that the richness and variety of archetypal images are such that it is difficult, if not impossible, to demonstrate that they are associated *exclusively* with behaviour having survival value.

Indeed, among the archetypes there is one of particular importance for religion and religious experience. As previously noted, religion has always been a universal phenomenon. It affects peoples everywhere and at all times. For instance, there is the widespread desire to be wed in church even when the couple are not normally noted for attending church. Even in countries where religion is officially discouraged, pseudo-religious rituals are observed. It does not take much imagination to see a parallel with the visit that newly wed couples in Moscow pay to the tomb of Lenin, or with the requirement to observe a reverential hush and remove one's hat on entering Chairman Mao's mausoleum in Beijing. As for countries where organized religion is not discouraged but appears to be on the decline, one finds that decline in part compensated for by a growth of interest in the occult, visitors from space, and so on.

The seemingly irrepressible urge to give expression to religious feeling indicated to Jung that it must have an archetypal basis. He associated it with an archetype of especial significance – one occupying a dominant position at the centre of the psyche (the psyche being the totality of the conscious and unconscious minds). This archetype is different from others in that all the other archetypes relate to it. It is called *the self*. This can be a little confusing in that the term as used here does not quite carry its normal meaning. Customarily 'self' is thought of as synonymous with 'ego'. In the present context, however, the self is defined as the centre of the entire thinking individual, embracing both the conscious and unconscious processes, together with the exchanges between the two. The ego, on the other hand, is specifically the centre of consciousness.

How does the ego react when it searches into the fathomless depths of the unconscious and is confronted by the self? It responds in a way very similar to, indeed indistinguishable from, that which was earlier spoken of as the inner experience of the numinous. Jung held that the discovery of one's inner self has the closest possible affinity to being confronted with the religious experience. The same characteristics of awe and wonder are there. There is an indissoluble link between the two activities.

What does this mean? It is held by religious believers that if one searches for God and succeeds in establishing a relationship with him, that discovery at the same time leads to the realization that there is a spiritual dimension to oneself. In other words, discovering God simultaneously deepens one's understanding of what it is to be human. What Jung appears to be proposing is that this process of discovery works both ways: discovering one's true inner self at the same time points to an experience of God.

The otherness of the mind

So where have we got to? Recall how we began this study of the mind in an attempt to understand why so many theologians believe that one finds God not by looking to the physical world but by seeking him in the very depths of oneself. We noted that the attributes of God are described exclusively in the language commonly used for the description of conscious mental phenomena. It therefore seemed reasonable to conduct an investigation that was to be carried out in that same language – an investigation into our personal experience of consciousness. We embarked on this even though it was unclear at the time how a study of one's own mind could reveal the existence of Someone who was not oneself.

We asked what kind of mind we would expect to find. As we have seen, the mind does not start off at birth as a blank – it has an inbuilt architecture. Evolutionary psychologists have enjoyed great success in accounting satisfactorily for many of these innate features of the mind as being the evolutionary adaptations of self-replicating survival machines. But that was not the whole story. Not all of our universal mental features could be accounted for as adaptations to meet identifiable demands to do with the survival and reproduction needs of our ancestors. This led to the suggestion that these additional features might have arisen as by-products of adaptations – what we have been calling spandrels. Providing these were neutral as regards survival, they might have become incorporated into the human genome as extra baggage.

In order for any feature to be reliably classed as a spandrel one needs to identify which adaptation or adaptations are likely to have spawned it. Thus one can happily account for our interest in sport in terms of the competition between our ancestors over gaining food and shelter, the need to channel aggression, the admiration of physical prowess once used in hunting, and so on. Many of the qualities of top-class athletes and sportsmen and -women were those required by our ancestors if they were to survive.

But then we came across other innate features that did not so readily lend themselves to explanation in terms of either adaptations or by-products. We spoke of the appreciation of beauty. Not just sexual beauty, for which a good case could be made for why we prefer certain characteristics in a mate, but also the beauty of flowers, a rainbow, and so on. There was the feeling of awe. There was the conviction that life has a purpose and that there is a moral law extending beyond that which can be reduced to mere reciprocal altruism or altruism on behalf of close kin. We noted the uplift to be derived from art, literature, music and the contemplation of nature, and the sense of accomplishment that arises out of being creative. There is the question of why we have feelings at all rather than experience a mere indifferent awareness of what is going on. There is the conviction that one possesses free will; one is not an automaton. In addition there are religious experiences.

Yes, there have been attempts to explain to a limited extent how activities such as making music might have come about. But these have hardly touched on the question as to why we react to them in the way we do – why some instances of them are regarded as aesthetically pleasing and others not. One can well understand why evolutionary psychologists are driven to do their best to offer explanations of as many features of the mind as they can, using the techniques they have developed. There are surely further advances to be made. However, especially in regard to the so-called by-products, it is difficult to see how their views on how they might have originated can ever be corroborated. Indeed, one might be pardoned for thinking that some of the attempts that have been made to explain away these features seem pretty arbitrary, not to say far-fetched.

One thing seems pretty clear: there are features of the mind we are born with that are difficult to explain in terms of their simply being what one would naturally expect were a self-replicating survival machine to become aware of itself. There is an otherness to the mind. This in turn raises the question as to how this otherness got there.

So is this where God comes into the picture? Let us be clear. Our search for God in our innermost being is not a search for two entities: our mind and something separate, namely God. All we discover there is our mind. What we are saying is that the workings of that mind have not only been shaped by our evolutionary origins, but they might also carry the imprint of the Creator of that consciousness. It is through the study of the characteristics of that imprint – that otherness – that we get to know the nature of the God responsible for it.

The roots of belief

It is all very well saying that God might be ultimately responsible for these extra features, but what kind of God are we talking about?

Humankind's understanding of the nature of God has undergone a long and tortuous history. Here I have particularly in mind the major religions of the Abrahamic tradition, namely Judaism, Christianity and Islam. Our ancestors sought God by trying to make sense of the often puzzling and contradictory events of life. With there being so many diverse features of life it was initially surmised that there must be several gods, each with their own particular characteristics and interests, these often coming into conflict with each other, giving rise at times to seeming chaos.

One of these gods was called Yahweh. He was a territorial God, living up Mount Sinai. He came to an agreement, or covenant, with a particular tribe – the Israelites. From then on he became a tribal god. He would fight for them, provided they worshipped only him, he being jealous of the other gods. He went wherever his people went. He cared only for them. He thought nothing of killing off the first-born Egyptian children. He helped his wandering people to take over the lands belonging to the Canaanites, presumably because he had no regard for the rights of other peoples belonging to other tribal gods.

But given time, this perception of Yahweh was to change. This was largely due to the insights of a series of prophets. Elijah came to the conclusion that Yahweh was not exclusively a warlike god. One could pray to him in times of peace, when, for example, there was a need for rain to water the crops the Jews had planted. Rain comes from clouds. Clouds spread out across the whole sky and cover all land, so Yahweh's supposed domain of influence spread until he was regarded as being in charge everywhere, not just one mountain or one country. And if he was in charge of everywhere it was because it was his creation. Yahweh had now become the great Creator God – the God who had created the whole world. As such, all peoples belong to him. He was no longer confined to being the god of a particular tribe.

Later still, the peasant Amos had the insight that God, being the god of all peoples, was as much concerned with lowly, humble people such as himself, as he was with kings, princes and other rulers and leaders of nations. Hosea, through finding that he could forgive his wayward wife, discerned that God was not the fearsome vengeful deity he had until then been thought to be. He was a God who could love deeply even to the extent of being able to forgive sins and be merciful.

At a time when the Israelites were taken into captivity and exiled from their homelands, it was Jeremiah who insisted that God had not been left behind; one did not have to worship him exclusively in the Temple in Jerusalem; he was still with them and could be worshipped in their hearts.

Then, finally, for Christians at least, there came the perfect personification of God in human form through Jesus Christ. He did not originate the two greatest commandments, namely to love God with all one's heart, soul, mind and strength, and to love one's neighbour as oneself. These had already by then been accepted. Rather, Christ demonstrated both by his life and his death what it meant to live wholly according to God's wishes. As he claimed, anyone who had seen him had seen the Father.

And, one might add, this process of continually refining one's understanding of God goes on into our own times. One has only to think of changes in attitude that have recently taken place regarding the status of women and relationships between homosexuals.

As I said, this progressive coming to know God took a long time. Unravelling that sequence takes some doing because the writings of the Bible are not in chronological order. The Bible begins, for instance, with a description of the great God creating the world. But as we now recognize, that was quite a late insight – a much later account than, for example, the story that immediately follows in Genesis depicting God walking in the garden in the cool of the evening. It is only when the writings of the Bible are placed in the order in which they were written that one comes to recognize how much progress was made in coming to a consensus as to what God is really like.

And what we find is that the nature of the God we have ended up with resonates very closely with those extra features we have found in our own minds. Thus, for example, God created the world; we get satisfaction from being creative. God has feelings of sadness, pain, anger, and so on; we too have feelings. God has a purpose in mind in that he wants his people to know him and love him; we are convinced that our lives too could and should have purpose. God loves and is compassionate towards everyone; we too have the ability of expressing unconditional love to all, not just to close kin. God is good and hates evil; we too have a moral sense. God, through his Son, is self-sacrificing; we too feel compelled at times to be self-sacrificing, even if necessary to the point of death. God has the freedom to act according to his will; we too, despite what we might conclude from the apparently deterministic behaviour of our physical selves, have been given an experience – illusory or otherwise – of what it is like to have freedom of action, with the concomitant sense of personal responsibility for those actions.

These are the characteristics that make up the otherness of our minds – those features that are hard to account for in terms of evolutionary psychology. They have a certain quality about them. They are features that are highly desirable. To put it bluntly, if somewhat simplistically, we humans are a darned sight nicer people than we have any right to expect to be – given our origins! Not everyone all the time, of course. History, to say nothing of our own times, has many examples of people displaying appalling brutality and nastiness. Faced with such atrocities we instinctively react by accusing the perpetrators of 'behaving like animals'. In doing so, we are in effect admitting that, given the same circumstances, this is how we ourselves would expect to behave if in truth we were nothing but evolved animals. But that is not the way we are – at least not to the same extent. On the whole, we possess and display characteristics that are moral, noble, kind, loving and wholesome. That being so, it is but a short step to conclude that the source of such finer qualities, God, must similarly be so endowed.

It is no coincidence that these desirable qualities characteristic of God are embodied in those buildings built to the glory of God – cathedrals, mosques, synagogues and temples. They incorporate architecture that is lofty and awe-inspiring; there is the splendour of the vestments worn by the priests who are the representatives of God; there is uplifting music, the beauty of the language used, and of the art work symbolizing the presence of God. There is the sense within those who worship there that they have a calling to serve the needs of the wider community.

It is the close similarity between the qualities attributed to God, on the one hand, and the characteristics of the otherness of conscious experience, on the other, that suggests that those extra characteristics of the mind we are born with have been imprinted by God. *That at least from now on is going to be our assumption.*

In this regard we would do well to note an uncanny resonance between this conclusion and the mythical account of our origins to be found in Genesis. There we learn from the part of the story concerning the taking of the forbidden fruit by Adam (the Hebrew word Adam denoting humankind in general) that we are basically selfish and are quite prepared to take what does not belong to us; we are inclined to put ourselves first. This accords well with our evolutionary tendencies to give priority to our survival. But then to offset this somewhat harsh feature of human nature there comes the statement that we are nevertheless made in the image of God; we have the potential to be like God. Genesis is pointing out that we have this twofold nature – much like the twofold nature we have discovered in our study of the mind.

But if this is so, immediately we are faced with a problem: if our internal examination of consciousness has not brought us directly in contact with God, but just with his supposed effects on our mind, how were such thoughts and attitudes transmitted into the mind from God. Are we supposed to believe that they come from outside by some kind of telepathic link from a God situated up there in heaven, or somewhere out there?

No. Such thinking is naive. Earlier we noted that the theologian Paul Tillich described God as the Ground of All Being. At the time, we were enquiring as to why the physical world existed. And coupled to the idea of the world coming into existence, there was the further question of what sustains it in existence. At that time, we were asking these questions solely of the *physical* world. We concluded that, if these questions were meaningful, such a source of an impersonal world might itself be an agency that was impersonal. The argument for there being an ultimate source did not in any way have to point to a god who was consciously interested in each individual – the type of god for which we were seeking evidence.

However, if God is to be regarded as the Ground of *All* Being – note the word 'All' – then one has to take into account the totality of existence. In particular, one has to recognize that *consciousness* also exists. Consciousness, like physicality, needs an explanation for its existence. God must therefore be the source not only of that which is physical but also of consciousness. Furthermore, besides being the reason why consciousness came into existence, God also fulfils the function of sustaining it in existence.

But given that the Ground is the ultimate source of our consciousness, does this not imply that the Ground itself must have at least some sort of affinity to consciousness? Call it a Super Mind if you wish, though that is almost certainly too crude. That would be to treat God as one more existent conscious entity (albeit of a superior form) rather than the means by which conscious entities exist.

The manner in which consciousness is applied to God is probably way beyond what we humans can put into words. We can but use analogies. For example, take the case of someone who has a thought. She decides to write it down. What is written is not itself a thought; it is but ink marks on paper. Nor is the thought in the person's head to be regarded as ink marks writ large – obviously. Yet it is the thought in the person's mind that is responsible for the existence of the written sentence, and in turn the written sentence manifests the thought.

In the same way we might expect an examination of our consciousness to reveal something of the nature of consciousness as it might be applied to God, without our necessarily advocating that God has a mind much like ours only better. Indeed, with the Ground being capable of giving rise to creatures that are aware, it all but forces us to accept that it would itself possess awareness of a sort – an awareness of everything it had created. At the very least we might conclude that it is more appropriate to consider God to be conscious than it would be to regard God as not.

In the same vein, we can further argue that if in addition the Ground of All Being is capable of giving rise to persons, we must surely expect this Ground to incorporate personhood of a sort within itself.

Given this to be the case, we return to the question of how we would expect God, in his capacity as being the Ground of consciousness and personhood, to communicate to our minds and thus help to shape who we are.

We know the means by which our minds are influenced by the minds of other people. This exchange of thoughts is conducted not through any direct telepathic link but through the medium of the physical world. It is accomplished through talking, writing, and so on. You have a thought or an idea; you translate it into writing or speaking; I read what you have written or hear the sounds you have made; I decode the message; it ends up as a thought or idea now incorporated into my own mind. As we shall be seeing in the third and final part of this book, God can also use the physical world as a means of transmitting thoughts into our mind. But that does not concern us at the present stage of our discussion. What we have to understand is that God does not *need* the physical world as a medium for transmitting thoughts and messages. And no, I am not falling back on the kind of telepathic link from outside that I mentioned earlier. God is able to communicate with us at a much more basic level. As the Ground of All Being, none of this is necessary. As the very means by which the mind is held in existence, God has a *unique, direct link* into our consciousness.

Perhaps an analogy will be helpful: consider a plant rooted in the ground. Its characteristics are governed by those inherited from the earlier bulb or seed from which it was grown. In the same way, many of the characteristics of the mind are shaped by what was passed on to us by our parents in our DNA (and hence collective unconscious). Just as the plant is affected by external happenings – buffeted by the wind, being pruned by a gardener, irradiated by the Sun – so our mind is affected by external experiences. But of immense importance as far as the plant is concerned is its relationship to the ground in which it is embedded. It is from the earth the plant draws life-giving and sustaining water. Without the earth it would not survive. The earth sustains it. So it is with the relationship between our mind and the Ground of consciousness. Without that ground it would not survive.

But the analogy does not end there. We note that a plant's roots draw up not only the basic necessity of water, but also nutrients. It is nutrients that allow the plant to be truly healthy, to flourish, to fulfil its potential, rather than merely exist. Furthermore, what the plant draws from the earth can markedly affect its characteristics. For example, the colour of the petals of a hydrangea depends on the acidity of the soil. If the soil is acid, the colour will be blue; if it is alkaline it will be pink. It all depends on the uptake of aluminium from the soil.

In the same way the Ground of All Being not only creates and then keeps our conscious mind in existence, helping it to flourish, but is also able to pass up into that mind thoughts that mould its very nature – its otherness – all those features of the mind that one would not expect to be there if it were the mind of an evolved animal and nothing more.

Whether the qualities so offered are embraced and incorporated into the psyche depends on the individual. They might be absorbed into one's being; they might be rejected. Evil people such as Hitler and those running the death camps of the Holocaust clearly suppressed these finer feelings. Mother Teresa, on the other hand, provides an example of someone who welcomed them.

But as we have previously argued, one does not need to be religious, like Mother Teresa, in order to lead a decent, moral life. Atheists are perfectly capable of having a moral sense. Indeed, on occasion their basic decency, their efforts in support of good causes, and so on, might outshine those of certain religious believers. Moreover, they appreciate beauty just as much. They possess free will and have feelings. Their general experience of life can be equated to that of believers, with the exception of those experiences specifically associated with religion – the sense of the numinous and so forth. How do we account for this?

By way of response we point out that just because they do not *acknowledge* God does not mean they are not in contact with him. It is God who gives existence to their consciousness just as much as he does to that of believers. Thus God is able to implant into them all the non-religious features of the mind that are hard to explain in terms of evolutionary history. But instead of questioning where such features come from, atheists, in effect, simply see these features as a natural part of who they themselves are. After all, these feelings and sensations are there in their own mind and therefore seem to be a part of them. It is something they own and identify with.

In this way, idealistic non-religious humanists incline to the view that we are *naturally* good. We become corrupted only in later life – that corruption coming from society. But what are the grounds for believing in this natural goodness, given our ancestral background rooted in the so-called struggle for survival? And how come society is such a bad, corrupting influence if it is entirely made up of individuals who are all naturally good?

In contrast, the religious believer affirms that we start off in a very imperfect condition – possessing what is sometimes known as 'original sin'. It is then up to the individual to repent (meaning change their mind) and consciously re-centre their life on God. This entails acknowledging that all our desirable qualities emanate from the Ground, and that we are called upon to live by these adopted qualities even though sometimes this outlook on life comes into conflict with the basic instincts stemming from one's evolutionary past.

This relationship between ourselves and God is two-way. Not only do thoughts and mental dispositions arise out of the Ground of consciousness, but through prayer we can transmit our own thoughts down to that Ground. *It is in recognizing that we have entered into this relationship with God that we come to know God.*

3

Retracing steps

The final stage of our journey

Recall that we began with a quotation from Immanuel Kant: he said that it was possible to experience God, but only if one already knew God. That raised the question as to how one should get to know God in the first place. As we have discovered, getting to know God is bound up with this recognition that our minds are not mere carbon copies of our physical selves in psychological form. In addition they carry the imprints God has added to our psyche – those features we would not have expected to find there if we were nothing more than self-replicating survival machines.

But does such an acceptance of God rest *entirely* on our interpretation of those characteristics of mental experience that were hard to account for otherwise? By no means. As Kant said, once one 'knows' God then it opens up the possibility of having experiences of him. This I interpret as meaning that not only are we able to learn of him from our inner mental life, we may also have experiences of God through life in general, and in particular through reflecting on the nature of our encounter with the physical world. Such external encounters provide confirmatory evidence for the kind of God who has made his presence known to us in our inner being.

Let me be clear. Earlier we came to the conclusion that an examination of the physical world does not lead to incontrovertible proof of God's existence – the kind of proof that would satisfy a sceptic. That still stands. What we are now saying is that, setting aside the sceptical stance and adopting instead the approach of a believer – one who knows through introspection the kind of God we are dealing with – we are now in a position to view the world in a different light. In doing so, we find that our experiences of the physical world lend themselves to the interpretation that God is indeed revealing himself through that world. Earlier we saw how some people have tried, unsuccessfully, to find God in the gaps in our knowledge of the world. Now, by contrast, we seek him in what we do know about the world. We are asking whether the world betrays a veiled Presence. In other words, has God imprinted his characteristics on the physical world in much the same way as he has done on our minds? Does it resonate with the kind of God revealed in the otherness of the mind? Indeed, we study the world not just to enquire after confirmatory evidence for what we have already learned, but to see if it is able to deepen and enrich our understanding of God. It has also to be added that we need to check that there are no contraindications; that is to say, features about the world that contradict the view we have so far formed of the nature of God.

Why a world?

But before examining what kind of world we live in, we must first ask why there should be a world in the first place.

So far we have described God as the source of consciousness. Indeed, we have effectively *defined* God to be whatever is responsible for the phenomenon of consciousness. God is its Creator. That being so, when considering the physical world, it seems reasonable to conclude that, rather than postulating a second creative agency, the world also owes its existence to this Creator. We repeat: God is the Ground of *All* Being. This appears especially likely given that we know of the very close correlation between our mental experiences and what goes on in that part of the physical domain we identify with the brain.

But what motivated God to create the world in the first place? The answer lies in recalling how one of the unexpected features of our consciousness is the sense of fulfilment and pleasure we experience in creating something. As we saw, it might be through the production of a painting, the building of a piece of furniture, the making of a flower arrangement, the preparation of a special meal, the decoration of a room, the design of a garden or the birth of one's child. From our own experience we learn that the urge to create goes far beyond the need to create objects useful for reproduction and survival. Much that we enjoy creating serves no utilitarian purpose.

Might we not, therefore, conclude from this that God himself probably has similar motives for creating something? Why did he go to all the bother of creating a universe? He found it fulfilling. And being the kind of God he is, he wanted us to share in that type of experience. That is why we ourselves get so much satisfaction from our own small forays into being creative.

Indeed, the matter goes deeper. There is a strand of modern theology that describes us humans as co-creators with God. When we look at the world we cannot help but recognize that all is not as it should be. In so many respects conditions in the world fall short of the ideal. It is unfinished business. We feel compelled to do our bit to build a better world. Believers and non-believers alike feel this compulsion; we are all made in God's image. The difference is that religious people consciously believe they are working alongside their God in his continuing creative enterprise.

Closely allied to creativity, another feature of the otherness of the mind was the sense of purpose. Though there is nothing in our description of the workings of the physical world that requires us to introduce the notion of purposefulness – everything happening in a deterministic fashion – yet we feel that our lives are invested with a sense of aiming at chosen goals. Is this a clue that God has a sense of purpose?

We recall that the God we have come to know is primarily a God of love. But for love to be exercised there must be someone to love. Might that therefore be a further reason for God to create the world? It was not just about the satisfaction to be derived from the act of creating something. God wanted to create someone to love, namely ourselves and any other intelligent beings throughout the universe. The physical world was to be our home. And because he wanted to allow for the possibility of that love to be returned, he created us with minds that could love. That was his purpose – his overall aim.

His purposefulness manifests itself in another way. Once one accepts that there is a spiritual dimension, there comes the realization that life can have an overarching purpose. Not one of those purposes one has consciously decided for oneself, but one that has seemingly been imposed from beyond. Life assumes a certain pattern. I am sure most of us on occasion experience confusion about what is happening to us, especially if it involves suffering or loss. We ask why a supposedly good and benevolent God would allow such troubles to occur. It is only with the benefit of hindsight that one might come to recognize that these setbacks are part of a plan that works out well in the end. Yes, it is painful to go through a divorce, for instance, but it is only through that first-hand experience that one becomes sensitized as to how best to minister, on God's behalf, to those who are going through the same trial. Time and again in the Bible we read how some called to be great prophets had not wanted to assume such a prominent and sometimes dangerous vocation. It was thrust upon them. Recall how Moses protested to God that he was not suited for such a role because he did not have the gift of persuasive speech. But he had to go through with it. He was an integral part of God's plan for the Israelite people. Then there was the case of Jeremiah. God told him, 'Before you were born I set you apart and appointed you as my prophet to the nations.' Before he was even born! Jeremiah's future was already mapped out for him. And in our own small way, we too can feel that we are being compelled to act in a manner that is counter-intuitive, but somehow does seem for the best in the end.

The believer accepts that this is further evidence that God has a purpose in mind for us. Like creativity, a sense of purpose is very much an integral characteristic of God. And in making us in his own image, he endowed us too with our individual capacity to live purposeful lives rather than live in a resigned state of helpless inevitability when faced with the spectre of determinism.

Closely allied to the notion of purpose is that of free will. There is no point in having a purpose unless one has the freedom to choose that aim for oneself, and the ability to work towards its accomplishment. When previously we were studying the contents of our minds, we noted that, among the features we would not have expected to find there if the conscious experience was merely that of a deterministic survival machine, was the conviction that we had free will. Treating this as an imprint from God we conclude that God himself is capable of making free choices – a conclusion that appears to be confirmed when recognizing that, where the creation of the physical universe was concerned, choices among various possible alternatives were needed. These included whether there should be a universe at all, what kind of universe it should be, and whether to include conscious living creatures.

What kind of world?

So much for why there should be a world. Given that it exists and is the handiwork of God, we move on to study its characteristics. It is only reasonable to assume that features associated with the Creator might manifest themselves in what is being created. This is in much the same way as the characteristics of a painting often tell us something about the kind of person responsible for it. There is, for instance, a world of difference between the tortured nature of the works of Van Gogh, such as *Wheatfield with Crows*, and the tranquillity of Monet's many depictions of water lilies. Van Gogh is believed to have committed suicide at age 37, dying of gunshot wounds; Monet was not so troubled and lived to a ripe old age of 86.

So what might we learn about God from the study of his creation? Bearing in mind the benign nature of the God who we are assuming is responsible for the features of the otherness of the mind we have discovered, let us see if there are traces of the same to be found in nature.

Design or many worlds

The first thing to note about the world is something very basic, namely that it is capable of sustaining life. In our earlier discussion of the anthropic principle we saw that the universe at first sight presents us with what seems to be a very hostile environment. Only a few isolated locations, such as planet Earth, are conducive to life. It is perhaps not the sort of world we ourselves would have created if our main aim was simply to provide a home for life. And yet closer examination led to the conclusion that if any number of its features had been slightly different from what they are, life for one reason or another would have proved impossible. It seems as though the world has been fine-tuned in order to accommodate us.

At the time, I warned against trying to use this observation as a proof that there must have been a Divine Designer. We know what happened to the attempt to use the 'design' of the human body as the basis for such an argument. And sure enough, just as Darwin's theory of evolution undermined the earlier argument, so scientists have come up with a possible alternative explanation of the anthropic principle: the multiverse. This is the suggestion that there are many other universes – perhaps an infinite number – and they are all run on different lines, with just the occasional freak universe, such as our own, having by chance the characteristics required for the development of life.

While this is clearly a possibility, one needs to be clear that whereas there is a wealth of evidence to back up the theory of evolution, there is none at all to confirm the multiverse hypothesis. Indeed, it is difficult to see how the other universes, which by definition are not part of our own universe, could ever be accessed and their reality thus confirmed. Belief in them must rest on the seeming plausibility or otherwise of theories currently being devised setting out possible mechanisms for producing a plethora of universes. But theories not backed up by evidence do not count as science.

So what is it to be: a single uniquely designed universe on the one hand, or an infinite number of diverse universes on the other?

Those inclined to atheism have little choice but to put their faith in the multiverse. Religious believers have a choice. They might be inclined to prefer the former alternative as being the simpler solution, the latter seeming somewhat extravagant. But not necessarily so. We know that God's adoption of the evolutionary process for producing us humans also gave rise to a rich abundance of other living creatures. Though God was presumably mainly interested in producing intelligent creatures that could enter into a relationship with him, he doubtless, like us, also takes delight in all the other animals and plants the creative process has brought forth. In the same way, God might well have adopted an analogous procedure for bringing our universe into existence alongside a great many other universes – variants that, while not of themselves containing life, might nevertheless be a source of delight to God.

Awe and beauty

A further feature of the inner life is the sense of the numinous. We have spoken about its awesome nature; it provokes in us what is sometimes called 'godly fear'. This does not mean it is frightening in the ordinary sense of the word 'fear'. Quite the contrary. The presence is benign and caring. Not only that, but our answers to prayer are generally understood to be reassuringly in our best interests. Nevertheless, the presence of the numinous does provoke a profound sense of respect and reverence – the kind of respect one might feel bound to show to a monarch. So do we find this awesomeness reflected in nature?

Without a doubt. On contemplating the universe, we immediately find ourselves confronted by the realization that God works on a different scale from us. Take, for example, the question of time. As is well known, the universe was created in a Big Bang. The stars so produced are gathered together in great swirling whirlpools called galaxies. Our own star, the Sun, is a member of the Milky Way galaxy. On observing the galaxies, one finds that they are still speeding away from each other in the aftermath of the Big Bang. By measuring their speeds and allowing for how these would have varied over time, we can calculate how long it must have taken for the galaxies to have reached their current positions. This yields an estimate of 13.8 billion years for the age of the universe.

Such a span of time defies the imagination. Given that God intended eventually to create consciousness in ourselves, and possibly in other creatures throughout the universe, we see that he works to a timescale very different from our own. This being so, perhaps this is telling us that we ourselves in our own lives could well adopt a different perspective as regards time, and practise more patience.

Then there is the question of size. Everything about the universe is big. The Sun is big enough to swallow up a million Earths. And yet, as already mentioned, it is but a star much like all the other stars. There are 300 billion stars in our galaxy, and there are 100 billion galaxies in the universe. Current estimates of the total number of stars in the universe stand at 70 billion trillion (7×10^{22}). And that is just the observable universe. Because it takes time for light to reach us from distant objects, we can observe only those galaxies that are close enough for their light to have reached us in the 13.8 billion years that the universe has existed. This is called the observable universe. Beyond that, who knows how many galaxies there are in the universe as a whole. Nor do we necessarily stop there. As we have just been discussing, there could be universes other than our own.

Contemplating such figures creates in us a sense of awe. Reacting in such a manner to creation, we are led as a consequence to some appreciation of how awesome its Creator must be. Earlier we mentioned in connection with the mental experience of the presence of the numinous that such a presence contained some hint of awesomeness. Now, confronted by the immensity of the physical universe, we find that sense confirmed.

Closely associated with the experience of awe is the appreciation of beauty. We have seen that that too was a feature of our conscious experience, which was not always easy to explain in terms of being relevant to survival and reproduction. It is all too easy to take for granted that the world we live in contains many things that are considered beautiful – rainbows, flowers, trees, sunsets, snowy mornings, and so on – to say nothing of the beauty that mathematicians and scientists see in their equations and theories.

It need not have been so. The world could have been unremittingly ugly and brutal. Human existence could have been sheer misery. It takes little effort to dream up an odious God who might have created such a world simply because that reflected his own despicable nature. For someone who has come to know God in their own inner life, and who recognizes that the ability to appreciate beauty in nature is a gift from God, the sheer beauty of so much in the world speaks volumes as to the nature of its Creator.

The laws of nature

The world is not chaotic. At first sight it might seem so. Our early ancestors must have often found the world they lived in very unpredictable and quixotic. But over the course of time all that changed. We now recognize that everything that happens does so for a reason. Each event is a link in an orderly, predictable chain of cause and effect governed by the operation of a few elegant laws of nature.

Not that it has been easy to come to this realization. The discoveries of scientists have been hard won. Discerning the basic simplicity underlying the bewildering variety of nature requires intelligence. And that in turn raises an interesting question, namely: if it takes intelligence to work out that there are laws of nature, might it not have taken an Intelligence to create the laws in the first place? This would be a conclusion that fits in naturally with the suggestion that there is a God, those laws being a reflection of the orderliness and dependability of the mind of the Creator.

Order and disorder

According to Greek mythology, before the creation of the world there was chaos. Likewise, the book of Genesis speaks of a beginning that was formless; there was a watery deep over which the spirit of God moved. It seemed natural to ancient people that if something came into existence it would at first be shapeless; it would require some agency to develop it into something more distinctive. Indeed, we know that with the world the way it is there is a tendency for it to revert to chaos. One of the laws of nature is the second law of thermodynamics. This holds that entropy – that is to say, disorder – increases over time. A cup hitting the kitchen floor breaks; food decays; milk goes sour; the house requires continual cleaning; cars end up as wrecks; the Sun will eventually burn itself out; our bodies gradually wear out; death is unavoidable.

The reason for this is that there are far more disorderly states than orderly ones. Imagine you are shown two pictures. One depicts a tall factory chimney and the second is a pile of rubble. You are asked which came first: the intact chimney or the rubble? The answer is obvious. Rubble does not come together to create chimneys but chimneys can collapse and become rubble. There is only a very limited number of configurations of the bricks that make up a chimney but there is an unlimited number of configurations of those bricks that constitute a pile of rubble. So if one state is going to develop into another state, the latter has a much bigger chance of being an example of rubble rather than an example of a chimney. Hence the photograph of the ordered chimney is likely to have been taken first.

And yet all is not gloom and doom. The world is such that, against this overwhelming tide carrying everything towards chaos and disorder, there can be small pockets swimming in the opposite direction. Old chimneys are demolished but new ones are built to take their place; cups break but new ones are manufactured; stocks of food are replenished; cars in the showroom replace those in the scrapyard; old people die, but babies are born.

It is important to stress that none of this defies the second law's inevitable march towards disorder. This becomes clear when one takes into account the bigger picture. By that I mean that all these activities ultimately depend, in one way or another, on the constant receipt of energy from outside. Ultimately we are talking about light and heat from the Sun. And the Sun, as it burns up its fuel in its great fires, is creating so much disorder that if we consider what is happening in the combined system of Sun-plus-Earth we would find that, overall, there would be a net increase in disorder in accordance with the law.

Not that there is any mystery over the fact that there can be these pockets of order working against a sea of disorder – a feature of the universe essential to our own existence. Scientists can undoubtedly account for it in terms of the ordinary working of nature. But it does strike me at least as extraordinary that the world is such as to allow such a thing to happen. If a human were set the task of designing an imaginary world and he or she came up with such a suggested scheme of things, it would be regarded as an act of genius.

The same goes for the workings of the human body and its powers of self-healing. We perhaps take it for granted that if we cut our finger all we have to do is put on a plaster to keep the dirt out, and it will in time heal. On breaking one's leg, a surgeon might be required to set the bones and put the leg in plaster, but from then on it is the body itself that finishes the job of healing. This self-healing does not, of course, apply to everything that might go wrong with our bodies – cancer, for instance. But is it not remarkable that the body can to any extent at all swim against the tide leading to things going wrong? After all, what things made by humans – cars, washing machines, hair dryers – have any ability to put themselves right when they go wrong?

The ingenuity of the physical world shows itself in another way: at its most basic level matter is composed of simple electrons and quarks. The quarks together form neutrons and protons. Neutrons and protons form nuclei. Nuclei and electrons form atoms. Combinations of atoms give rise to molecules. It is at the molecular stage that something very peculiar emerges. If the shape of the basic building blocks of the universe had been simple round balls or cubes, and these came together to form larger structures, that is, 'molecules', these larger structures could take any random shape. The whole ensemble would, quite frankly, end up a mess. But things are not like that in this world. Its molecules are such that they have definite characteristic shapes. The water molecule, for instance, consisting of one atom of oxygen joined to two atoms of hydrogen, is such that the angle between the bonds linking the two hydrogens to the oxygen is always 104.5 degrees. It is never some other angle. And the same applies to other types of molecule; they each have their own characteristic structure. Moreover, these molecules can come together to produce even more elaborate structures, such as the helical form of the DNA molecule.

Again I hasten to say that scientists have a ready explanation of this in terms of the natural working out of the laws of nature. These shapes of atoms and molecules can be understood as arising out of the workings of quantum theory – the theory governing the behaviour of small entities such as atoms. Nevertheless, on reflection, one cannot but be impressed by this extraordinary self-organizing feature of the world. As with the existence of pockets of order we came across, might this not also hint at some underlying Intelligence at work?

Timelessness

One of the features commonly attributed to God is that he transcends time. God certainly works within time, as for example when we engage with him in prayer, but additionally, unlike ourselves, God is not confined by time. According to our human view of time, the past has ceased to exist; the future has yet to exist; all that exists is the present. But that is not how it is with God. Theologians hold that from his vantage point – whatever that might be – God has access to all of time. In particular he knows the future. It is not a question of God being capable of making a better-informed guess than ourselves as to what the future might hold. He *knows* the future.

This belief is founded on taking seriously various passages of the Bible. We have already come across one example of this when we recounted the story of Jeremiah being told by God that his future as a prophet had already been decided before he was born. In addition we have both St Peter and St Paul writing of God's foreknowledge. Jesus spoke with complete conviction about his forthcoming crucifixion and resurrection. Likewise, the anticipated establishment of the kingdom of God is always spoken of as a fact, not merely as a pious hope. We have Jesus' enigmatic statement: 'Very truly, I tell you, before Abraham was, I am' (John 8.58). Scholars point out that this is primarily a statement that Jesus outranks Abraham. Nevertheless, it does also seem to imply that there is some ambiguity regarding Jesus in relation to time.

God's foreknowledge is a contentious issue. Some theologians – especially those known as process theologians – simply do not go along with it. They hold that until the future actually happens, knowledge of it is an impossibility. I suspect that might be your own gut feeling! Does an examination of the physical world throw any light on this subject? I believe so. To see how requires us to delve a little way into what Einstein's theory of relativity has to say about the nature of the world.

In speaking of God as the Creator, we were at pains to point out that this did not mean God was the cause of the Big Bang. A cause of the Big Bang would have to have preceded it in time. But where the Big Bang was concerned, according to relativity theory, it marked the coming into existence of time, as well as of space. So there was no preceding time to accommodate a cause. This in turn implies that the creative influence responsible for the world's existence, if we can call it that, must be coming from outside of time and space.

But how does relativity come to the conclusion that the connection between time and space is so intimate that with the expansion of space from nothing, implying that space came into existence at the Big Bang, so also did time?

Contrary to what one might instinctively think, we do not all inhabit the same space and time. If you are in an aeroplane flying overhead and I am on the ground, your space is squashed up compared to mine (this is known as *length contraction*), and time in your moving aeroplane runs more slowly than mine (*time dilation*). At the speeds we are talking about, the differences are so tiny that we are unaware of them. There is, for example, no need to reset your watch on landing to get back into synchronization with mine. But at high speeds – those approaching that of light, namely 300,000 kilometres per second, speeds reached by subatomic particles being whirled round particle accelerators such as the Large Hadron Collider at the CERN laboratory in Geneva where I used to work – the differences can be enormous.

So how are we to account for these differing spaces and times? The answer from relativity theory is that we are not dealing with a three-dimensional space and a separate one-dimensional time as is usually assumed. Instead, we inhabit a single four-dimensional reality called spacetime. Going back to the case of you being in an aircraft and myself on the ground, we disagree about both the separation in time and the separation in space of your departure from London and your subsequent arrival in New York. But we do agree about the separation of those two events in four-dimensional spacetime. This leads to the conclusion that what is real – what actually exists – is not space and time separately but this integrated spacetime. Space and time as we experience them are merely appearances of that reality from particular points of view. They are three-dimensional and one-dimensional projections respectively of the four-dimensional reality.

The fact that we disagree about the projections is no more significant than the manner in which a pencil can look long or short depending on our point of view relative to that object. In the case of the pencil, this difference over appearances does not bother us because we are aware that what we see with our eyes is no more than a two-dimensional projection of what in reality is a three-dimensional object. We are in agreement over what the length of the pencil is in three-dimensional space, and that is all that matters. It is this three-dimensional length that is the actual length of the pencil, not the two-dimensional appearances.

In the same way, we need to go beyond space and time viewed separately and concentrate on what the situation is in space-time. Hermann Minkowski, a former tutor of Einstein, declared, 'Henceforth, space by itself, and time by itself, are doomed to fade away into mere shadows, and only a kind of union of the two will preserve an independent reality.'

And what do we expect to find in this spacetime? Whatever it is must be characterized by a particular position in space, coupled with a particular instant in time. It might, for example, be the departure of your aeroplane from London, Heathrow (its position), at 1.30 p.m. on Thursday (its point in time). In other words, we are dealing with *events*. The contents of spacetime are events.

An important feature of spacetime is this: not only do all points in space exist at each point in time, something we are perfectly happy to accept, but also each point in time exists at each point in space. So, for instance, where you are sitting now reading this book, not only does this present instant exist, but also the moment you took up the book to start reading, and the moment when (doubtless thankfully!) you set it aside to do something else. All events – past, present and future – exist on an equal footing. A very counter-intuitive idea, I am sure you will agree, but a conclusion that appears to follow on inevitably from acceptance of the reality of spacetime.

Next we note that nothing ever changes in spacetime. Changes can only occur in time. But spacetime is not in time; time is contained within spacetime. Due to its unchanging nature, certain scientists refer to spacetime as the *block universe*.

Nothing can be more alien to our instinctive feelings than the block universe. Our conscious perception of reality is inescapably one of change. So how does that fit with the unchanging nature of the block universe? What seems to be happening is that our consciousness acts like a sort of searchlight beam progressively scanning along the time axis of spacetime, making us consciously aware of what occurs at just one particular point in time. We give a label to this point in time: 'now'. The searchlight beam then moves on to the adjacent point in time. The name 'now' is transferred to this new point. And so on, always moving in the direction towards that to which we give the name 'future'. Thus we consciously experience sequentially only the events associated with a single point in time. It takes a great leap of the imagination to recognize that this changing experience is a feature solely of our conscious perception of reality and not a property of the physical reality itself. I suppose it is somewhat analogous to the way we consciously experience free will, whereas the physical description of reality seems to exclude it.

The block universe seems so counter-intuitive that, just as some theologians refuse to accept God's foreknowledge, so also some physicists do not accept the block universe. As a physicist myself I do accept it – albeit somewhat reluctantly. I don't see the alternative. Maintaining that only those events happening at the present instant can exist has become untenable. This is because of a further consequence of relativity theory. This shows that if the two of us are moving relative to each other – you in the aircraft passing me overhead – while there is no problem over our agreeing about what is happening at this instant where we are both located, say in London, we do *not* agree as to what is happening at the present instant in, say, New York. Which in turn means we cannot agree about what *exists* at the present instant in New York. None of which is a problem for the block universe idea; *all* events exist in New York. According to the block universe idea, the disagreement is merely one of deciding which of the existent events in New York should carry the time label 'now'.

The outcome from this rather lengthy diversion into relativity theory is that if one accepts the block universe theory then it immediately becomes much easier to accept that God can indeed have foreknowledge. The objection to it was that it was impossible to know the future for certain until it happens – until it exists. But now we have good reason to believe that, in some sense (and don't ask me to elaborate in what sense!), the future does indeed exist. All God has to do is to gain access to it from his vantage point transcending space and time. I often think that as a physicist – one who fully accepts the findings of relativity theory – it is easier for me to believe in God's foreknowledge than it is for many a theologian. I count it as a classic case of gaining further insight into God's manner of thinking from a study of the physical world he has created.

Miracles

We have been attempting to learn something of God through a consideration of the laws of nature. But how about violations of those laws; that is, miracles? When previously we studied miracle accounts we did so from the point of view of the sceptic. We found there was nothing there that compelled a sceptic of a need to accept them at face value. This, for example, might have been on the grounds that there could have been some natural explanation for what happened. In the case of recovery from an incurable illness or disability, there could have been an initial wrong diagnosis. We needed to take into account that people living long ago took a positive delight in wondrous tales of mysterious happenings. Accordingly, in trying to get across spiritual truths they had no qualms about playing fast and loose with what might be scientifically plausible.

But now the situation is different. We are now assuming that one has become convinced, through the experiences of one's inner life, that there is a God, and that this God was the Creator of those laws of nature. From this perspective, it becomes reasonable to accept that the Creator of the laws had, and continues to have, the power to suspend those laws should he decide that circumstances called for it. It becomes no longer a question of whether miracles are possible; that is, whether God has the power to suspend the laws. The question is whether God does have sufficient reason, on occasion, to suspend them.

But if so, would not such interventions of necessity seem arbitrary and inconsistent? Not necessarily. Consider how the God encountered in one's inner life is a loving God – a God who takes a personal interest in one's well-being. We know what we would do if faced with a loved one in distress; we would do all in our power to help. Would that not be the same with this God of love? Would God not do all in his power to help those in need? Having the power to suspend the laws, would he not on occasion be obliged to exercise that right? Though at the physical level miracles are to be seen as violations of those laws, from a wider perspective such actions can be seen as perfectly in accord with an overriding higher law: the law of love.

If, as we shall later be discussing, Jesus was the Son of God, the perfect embodiment of love, then when faced with someone in need, he had no option but to help – using what supernatural powers he possessed if necessary. It should perhaps not surprise us that miracles were more prevalent at the time of Jesus' ministry than they are today. Not that this is an excuse to accept all the miracle accounts listed in the Bible, lock, stock and barrel. The previous criticisms of some of the accounts still hold. But the idea that there might be a higher law of love, and that Jesus was someone especially bound to exercise that law, makes it no longer surprising that certain of the biblical accounts might in fact relate to events that did happen literally as described.

Especially this is so of those miracle accounts illustrating some spiritual truth. At the feeding of the 5,000, for instance, Jesus speaks of his ability to satisfy a more important spiritual hunger. When curing a man born blind, he draws attention to the spiritual blindness of certain of the onlookers. He uses the miraculous haul of fish to illustrate how he had in mind for the fisherman the higher task of becoming fishers of people.

In summary, what I am saying is that, while there is no excuse for being gullible when it comes to the acceptance of biblical miracles, once one has come to know God in the manner we have been discussing, then it encourages one to be more open-minded on the subject. I suppose my own ingrained habitual type of thinking as a professional scientist inclines me to be particularly cautious over the acceptance of miracles. Nevertheless, I am comfortable with the view that for at least some of the miracles there were good spiritual grounds for accepting them.

And in this regard one should not just be thinking of miracle accounts dating back to biblical times. Though miracles might have been more frequent at the time of Jesus' ministry, for the reasons given, claims are still made today, particularly in regard to healing miracles. Some, as previously mentioned, might indeed arise through a misdiagnosis of the condition. But others are harder to dismiss. And why should they be dismissed out of hand? God's loving actions were presumably not confined to the three years of Jesus' ministry.

Communication through the physical

All the above relates to miracles in the narrow sense of their being violations of the physical laws. But strictly speaking, as we have already pointed out, in theological circles the word 'miracle' applies to *any* action that is particularly revelatory of God – whether or not it involves a violation of the laws. So far we have been looking at the world to see whether its various characteristic features offer clues as to the nature of its Creator. But does God additionally have something to reveal to us through certain particular events occurring in that world?

In Old Testament times this was very much thought to be the case. If, for example, there was some catastrophe such as a flood or a drought or a defeat in battle, this was regarded as God admonishing his people for their waywardness. If times were favourable with, for instance, abundant harvests, these were regarded as signs sent from God that he was pleased with them. In our own day we might hear of a miraculous escape from a car crash. This need not imply that we think that a law of nature has been suspended – a miracle in the narrow sense. But for someone who knows God, such a fortunate occurrence can well be regarded as God demonstrating his loving protection through the incident. Or perhaps by chance one happens to meet up with someone who later has some profound and beneficial effect on one's life. We might simply put it down to luck that we met in the first place. Alternatively, we might conclude that it was God who destined us to meet.

But if God is communicating to us in this manner, how is this possible? How can his mind communicate with our minds in this way if, as we have been describing, the workings of this world are already laid down in a deterministic fashion – one slavishly following the dictates of the laws of nature?

This raises the general question as to how one mind affects another. In our normal encounters with people, the meeting of minds is exclusively mediated through the interaction of physical bodies in the physical domain. Adhering to the view that there is nothing odd going on in the human brain (that is, it behaves like everything else in accordance with the laws of nature), we nevertheless have no difficulty in accepting that one mind can make itself known to another.

Normally, of course, we are barely conscious that this meeting of minds is being conducted through a physical medium. We do not think of it in those terms. It becomes second nature to think in terms of a direct line of communication between one's own mind and that of the other person. We habitually think of someone else's thoughts and feelings directly influencing one's own thoughts and feelings. It is only when we stop and think out the matter in detail that we come to accept that all mental transactions are, in the final analysis, physically mediated.

This being how we communicate one with another, why should God not do the same? If – discounting the possibility of telepathy – we have no need of a non-physical channel in order to communicate with someone else, why should God?

But, it might be countered, we communicate using our body. God does not have a body as such. True, but interactions between two human minds do not have to involve their bodies – at least not directly. When we look at a painting, listen to music, enter a building, see an advertisement on the television, walk down a street or read a book such as this one, we are all the time being influenced by the minds of others – those of the painter, the composer, the architect, the advertiser, the town planner and the author. All this without our having met them in the flesh. It is sufficient that we come into contact with their handiwork. If it is thus possible to influence one another through nothing more than the simple rearrangement of physical objects – applying paint to a canvas, ink to paper, and so on – how much easier it must be for God, the Designer and Creator of all physical things, to communicate with us through the physical world. God does not need a distinctive body. The whole of the created world is mapped on to him. He stands behind all things and uses all things to disclose himself to us.

That being the case, what does God actually *do*? If the laws of physics carry on regardless, is not God superfluous? In a sense, yes – the same sense as other minds are superfluous. After all, what do other minds *do*? As far as the behaviour of the human body is concerned – the body thought of purely as an object of physical interest – the answer is, nothing. The laws of physics take care of everything. But in another manner of speaking, one that recognizes the existence of minds, and where we ask different kinds of question, the answer is that minds do everything. It is the same with God. As far as the study of physics is concerned, he too is superfluous. But when it comes to other kinds of discussion – those founded on a prior knowledge of the mind of God based on experience of one's own inner life – then God is seen to be permeating the whole of existence and all that goes on in it.

Creation through evolution

Up to now we have been looking at the world to see whether we can see indications that God has left his imprint on it – indications that back up the conclusions we have drawn about God's nature as found in consciousness. But if we are to be honest, we have to face up to what, at least at first sight, appear to be counter-indications – features that are hard to reconcile with the picture we have so far formed of God. This is to be the subject of this and the next section.

We begin by examining the process of evolution by natural selection. Is it consonant with the idea that this was a loving God's chosen method of producing us humans and the other animals?

Being a scientist myself I have no alternative but to accept the theory; the evidence in its favour is overwhelming. Many Christians do not go along with it, preferring instead the Genesis account of Adam and Eve, taken as a literal description of what actually happened. Partly this is through a sense of reverence for Scripture; partly it is because they find it difficult to believe that something as complicated as the bodies of humans and the other animals could have arisen in such a fashion.

There is a third reason for their discounting evolution. This is the difficulty of reconciling God's loving nature with the sheer cruelty and suffering that is incorporated into the evolutionary process. The theory requires many individuals to die premature and often painful deaths. Only those lucky enough to possess favourable gene mutations should mate and pass on those advantageous genes to the next generation. Those possessing less advantageous genes have to be eliminated, and this before they reach an age where they can pass their inferior genes to the next generation. Even those lucky enough to have mated have eventually to die in order to make way for the next generation. Only so can a species develop further and become more sophisticated, culminating in ourselves. There is no doubt about it: evolution is harsh and unfair.

So why would a good, loving God of justice choose such a method for bringing into the world creatures that could enter into a loving relationship with him? To address this question we need to examine what the alternatives might have been.

Could he, for example, metaphorically have sat down at a drawing board, designed us and then assembled us atom by atom according to the blueprint? Possibly, but what would have been the result? A robot. Could the robot say, 'God, I love you'? Yes. But only if that was what God programmed it to say. Would that have been genuine love? Of course not. In order to be able to offer genuine love one has to have a certain measure of independence from the person being loved. Love has to be freely offered. There has to be the possibility that it will be withheld. But a robot has no such freedom. It is nothing more than what its creator has dictated that it should be.

Suppose there had been more than one creator god. We could then envisage a human created by one of these gods showing a preference for one of the other gods – one who had had nothing to do with its formation. Such a human might transfer their love and loyalty to the second god. A love like that does have a chance of being genuine as it has been offered from a position of independence. But of course that is not how things are. There is no multiplicity of creator gods. The one God has created everything; nothing exists independently of God. So this is no solution to the problem as to how we are to acquire the necessary degree of independence.

So what is God's solution? The answer is *chance*. Instead of meticulously and slavishly designing each and every feature of us, God instituted a procedure capable of producing us on his behalf, so to speak – a procedure that would incorporate an element of chance. It is the unpredictable random mutations to the genes that confer on us our own individual, distinctive characteristics.

But, one might argue, if the whole procedure is based on chance, how could God possibly know what the end product would turn out to be? On the face of it, without a proper plan, it would appear to be a recipe for producing a mess! Not so. This is where natural selection comes into its own. Yes, the variations to the genes are random, and indeed most of them are probably deleterious. But natural selection weeds out the poor ones, leaving only the advantageous ones.

In recent years evolutionary biologists have come to the realization of just how predictable the outcome of evolution can be. Start the evolutionary process over again, on some other planet perhaps, and creatures will emerge that in many respects resemble ourselves. For example, there is so much survival value in being able to see that creatures with eyes are almost bound to emerge. Indeed, in the course of evolutionary history here on Earth, different kinds of eyes have evolved independently of each other. There is, for instance, a world of difference between the compound eye of a fly and the camera-type eye of humans. But the same goal is achieved: they can see. The same goes for hearing, for the ability to run or to fly, for being intelligent, and so on. As the palaeontologist Simon Conway Morris has pointed out, all these and many other qualities were almost certain to emerge over the course of time. This feature of the evolutionary process is known as *convergence*.

Thus despite the element of randomness, God could rely on the process producing creatures that were intelligent enough to reflect on the meaning of life – whether or not it went further than just the daily round of keeping alive. Creatures would emerge that could relate to God. Moreover, by virtue of the measure of independence they had gained, they could love God with a genuine love should they so choose.

In summary, I think this is why God adopted evolution by natural selection as his method of making us. Yes, it involves suffering and death – topics we shall come on to – but I don't see how a God whose overwhelming priority is the fostering of genuine love had any viable alternative.

Evil and suffering

And so we face the general, age-old problem of evil and suffering. The evil of people cheating, lying, stealing, committing murder, sexually assaulting and bullying children, mugging, carrying out terrorist attacks, waging war. There is suffering – that inflicted by these deliberate evil actions, together with further instances of suffering arising from natural disasters such as floods, earthquakes, volcanic eruptions, avalanches, drought, disease.

Let us be clear from the start. There is no easy pat answer as to why a supposedly all-powerful, loving God would permit these things to happen. On the face of it, the existence of evil and suffering seems a clear indication that there is no such God. But as we shall discover, closer examination reveals that matters are more complicated than that – much, much more complicated and multifaceted.

We begin by asking whether evil is real. I know that sounds a silly question but, as a preliminary, one does have to take it seriously. Is it really true that there are two forces at work: good and evil? According to one point of view the answer is 'No'. Only goodness exists; evil is merely the absence of goodness. This is in much the same way as 'darkness' is not a real entity; it is simply the absence of light. Only light is real. 'Cold' is another of these negative qualities. It is an absence of heat. Heat is real; it is the energy of molecules jiggling about or the energy of the rays emitted by the Sun or a fire. Cold is nothing but an absence of these features. If this is how we ought to regard evil then it is not something God has created. All God has done is to create goodness.

It is a pretty neat way of getting out of the problem. It is certainly true that negative qualities can have all the appearance of being a force in their own right. We freely talk of putting on extra clothing to keep the cold out, rather than to keep the heat in. In the evening we might speak of the darkness closing in, rather than the light fading. Nevertheless, treating evil as merely an absence of goodness surely does not do justice to the sheer scale of certain evil acts – the Holocaust or the atrocities committed by Islamic terrorists, for example. No, evil is something we do have to regard as being just as real as goodness and something that therefore needs to be accounted for.

Some blame the devil. The devil is pictured as a fallen angel. He was created by God but rebelled against his Maker. It is the devil who brought evil into the world. Today we are inclined to dismiss the idea of there being a devil. The word conjures up a picture of horns, a tail and a red cloak. We treat him as a joke. In times past it was helpful for people to think of evil as personified, actively luring people into sin. It helped them to take temptation to do wrong seriously and hence resist it. But I suppose few today regard the idea of the devil as being something we have to take literally. In any case, if there is a devil whose prime purpose is the spread of evil, it was God who created the devil and so presumably carries some of the responsibility.

Are we being forced to the conclusion that God is not entirely good, as we have been assuming? The psychologist Carl Jung was of that view. According to him, there is indeed a dark side to God. Among the Jungian archetypes we possess there is one called the *shadow*. It embodies those aspects of the self that the ego rejects as evil, damaging or reprehensible. Jung claimed that the shadow was also a feature of God's personality. He wrote:

> The God I experienced is more than love; he is also hate, he is more than beauty, he is also the abomination... If the God is absolute beauty and goodness, how should he encompass the fullness of life, which is beautiful and hateful. Good and evil.

But let us not be hasty. Before accepting Jung's somewhat morally ambiguous type of God, there are further considerations to be examined.

Having discounted the idea of evil being nothing more than the absence of goodness, we nevertheless have to recognize that there is a close connection between the two. In order to understand evil as the absence of goodness, we had first to know what we meant by goodness. That remains true. Without goodness, we would not know what evil is. And the reverse is true: without evil, we would not know what goodness is.

It is an odd thing about words that to a large extent they gain their meaning by reference to their opposites. Suppose, for instance, we had been brought up all our lives imprisoned in a windowless building in which the only illumination was by sodium lamps similar to the familiar yellow sodium street lights. Everything we saw was a shade of yellow. Would we know what the word 'yellow' meant? No. In practice we understand what we mean by 'yellow' because we live in a world where objects are lit by white light, making some objects appear yellow, but others not. Under these circumstances we are able to say, 'These objects are yellow; those are not.'

As a further example, suppose you are trying to learn a foreign language and someone points to a chair and says a certain word for it. She then points to other chairs and again says the same word. Can you immediately conclude that this is the word for 'chair'? No. For all you know, it might mean 'furniture'. It is only when she points to the table, the sideboard, a stool and shakes her head that you can eliminate the possibility that this foreign word means 'furniture'.

Thus we find it is only by being aware of examples of things that are not described by the word, as well as things that are, that we come to understand the meaning of the word.

In the same way, we come to understand the meaning of 'goodness' only in contrast to the word 'evil'. A world without evil would be a world where the concept of goodness would have no meaning. Evil is the price we have to pay for goodness. It appears to be a logical necessity. Even a so-called all-powerful God must of necessity abide by this restriction.

The next point to note is that the distinction between what is good and what is evil is not always straightforward. Take the nuclear bomb. With its capacity for eliminating all life on Earth, it is widely regarded as the world's worst evil. But possession of a nuclear capacity acts as a deterrent to aggressors, and has probably averted World War Three. Certainly the loss of life at Hiroshima and Nagasaki was horrendous, but it did bring that war to a conclusion, with the consequent saving of many other lives.

Likewise, science has much to answer for: global warming, pollution, damage to the ozone layer, questions to do with cloning, genetically modified crops and the development of ever more sophisticated and destructive weapons of war. But to offset those we have the undoubted benefits that have come with science, especially medical science. It is as well to recall that only a few hundred years ago one had less than a 50–50 chance of surviving to one's teens. I might add that I myself am particularly grateful for the invention of the high-speed dentist's drill and its replacement of the old, juddering, nerve-shredding predecessor!

This blurring of the distinction between good and bad shows up in all walks of life. A company falls on hard times and the management decide the firm needs to downsize. Employees are made redundant. There are protests that the management is being hard-hearted, causing the harsh times that will now befall the unlucky ones and their families. But what was the alternative? The company being allowed to fold with the loss of all jobs?

Or take the dilemmas that often face a mother. Naturally she does not want to hurt or deny her child. But sometimes she is forced to. She knows that removing the sticky plaster from the cut finger will cause momentary pain, but someone has to do it. Yes, the child loves sugary drinks, but it is in the child's longer-term interests if she temporarily incurs the child's wrath at having to forgo such indulgences.

Pain is widely regarded as a useful warning against dangers. The pain of appendicitis, for example, is the signal to get oneself to hospital. A horrible taste can be an indication that one should have looked at the sell-by date on the can. Of course, not all such unpleasant experiences are helpful. What use is it to suffer from arthritic pain, or the pain associated with many other conditions and diseases of various sorts, when there is nothing one can do about them? Nevertheless, certain kinds of pain can be useful.

Then there is the pain and risk we willingly take on in pursuit of some higher objective. Athletes and other sportsmen and -women, for instance, generally do not like having to train. Yet they voluntarily put themselves through all kinds of painful and boring exertions. This they do in the knowledge that it is only by such disciplined actions that there can be any prospect of success. Skiers are prepared to risk breaking a leg in order to experience the thrill of their sport. Californians enjoy their sunny lifestyle despite the knowledge that they live on the San Andreas fault line with the ever-present threat that one day there will be another earthquake such as that which destroyed San Francisco in 1906.

In so many ways good ends are achievable only by painful means. If we decide to take on such risks, we ourselves must surely shoulder some of the blame if things go wrong. We can hardly blame God.

But let us return to the problem posed by those situations where there is a clear distinction between evil and goodness, and where suffering is unavoidable. Where does gratuitous evil come from if we are not to hold an all-loving God responsible for it? It is time to turn to what has come to be known as the *free-will argument.*

We begin by noting that if we were gods, in charge of making a universe, I am sure we would want the creatures living in that world to be happy. It seems only natural that we would want them to enjoy life and live it to the full rather than be miserable. It is not for nothing we find, enshrined in the American Declaration of Independence, the pursuit of happiness held to be one of the unalienable rights of citizens. So if that is the kind of world we would have created, we might unthinkingly expect God to have done the same.

But God did no such thing. He made no promises of happiness. His priorities lay elsewhere. For God, what mattered was not superficial happiness but love. Love was his sole concern. And that being the case, certain unavoidable consequences follow.

First, we must be given free will. This is something we have already touched on in our discussion as to why God chose evolution by natural selection as his method for creating us. We had to have a measure of independence from him in order that we could of our own free will offer him our love and loyalty.

What we did not mention at that time, however, is that for that freedom to be real there had to be instances where that freedom was misused to reject God. If the situation was such that theoretically everyone could reject him, but in practice it was unthinkable that anyone ever would, that would surely call into question how meaningful this so-called freedom actually was. It is the real possibility that love might be withheld that makes the offering of love so valued. We see this in human relations. A boy tells a girl that he loves her. She is delighted. But then she finds out that he says that to every girl he meets. It is now not the same. His declaration of love is devalued. For her to feel special he has to be seen to be rejecting others in her favour.

And so it is with our love for God. It is the fact that so many turn their backs on God that makes the loyalty of the faithful so valuable. And turning one's back on God – which is something we all do from time to time – is turning aside from the source of all goodness, and that is how we come to embrace the opposite, which is evil. So where does evil originate? It does not come from God; it comes from us. Evil exists not because God wishes it, but because in order to achieve his objective, which is purely to create love, he has no alternative but to allow us to create evil. I repeat: without evil there is no good; without rejection there is no love. Even an all-powerful God has to abide by these logical necessities.

Another point to note: in order for us to be able to exercise free will we must be able to anticipate what will be the likely outcome of any action we choose to take. The world we live in has to be law-like and predictable – as indeed it is. Not only that, the world is the common medium by which we individuals, through the use of our physical bodies, interact with each other. It is a world where it cannot bend its rules to fit the whim of some individual because that might infringe the interests of some other person – one who has just as much, or as little, right to have things their way. You might want sunshine because you are going on holiday; a farmer might want rain for his crops. The arena in which we jointly operate must be neutral; it must have a nature of its own.

But it surely follows that, with this being the case, we might from time to time fall foul of nature operating in this blind automatic fashion – hence natural disasters. Allowing such things to happen is another price that has to be paid once love is raised to be the highest priority.

Another requirement for there to be love is that there should be opportunities for demonstrating it. Obviously. But how is love demonstrated? By having good times together? Going to parties? Sitting in the cinema eating popcorn together? Lots of sex? Motherly cuddling of a baby? Such activities might indeed be features of a loving relationship. But they do not constitute proof of love. They are enjoyable activities in themselves; we might be engaging in them purely for our own self-gratification. Proof – actual proof – of love, on the other hand, is demonstrated through the way we are prepared to put ourselves out in attending to the needs of the other: how we behave in times of trouble; how we sacrifice our own interests to alleviate the suffering of the other.

We see this, for example, in the way a mother, desperately tired after a hard day, will nevertheless get up in the middle of the night to change the baby's nappy. A husband devotes himself to the care of his disabled wife who has suffered a stroke, rather than going off with another woman. Someone, deeply moved by the plight of those suffering from a natural disaster, makes a big donation they can hardly afford.

It is the extent to which we are prepared to set aside our own interests in order to meet the needs and alleviate the suffering of others that is the true measure of love. Of course suffering is to be avoided if at all possible, but when it happens it can be marshalled for good. It provides an opportunity for love to flourish. It brings people together. It deepens relationships.

Indeed, it is probably true to say that a world in which love is the highest priority is one where there has to be suffering also. After all, for Christians, how do we know that God loves us? Primarily by the sending of his Son to live with us and to endure great suffering on our behalf. Had Jesus lived a comfortable, privileged life, to a grand old age, living in a mansion in Surrey, playing golf on a Sunday, would we know for sure how he felt about us? Would our attitude towards him have been different? Of course it would.

There is one further thought regarding God as a God whose prime quality is that of love. We have earlier pointed out that theologians have long held that God as he is in himself is absolutely unknowable. When trying to describe God we have to fall back on metaphors and analogies. When, for example, we speak of God as our Heavenly Father we are saying that our relationship to God is something like our relationship with our earthly father. We do this fully accepting that there are, nevertheless, aspects where the similarity breaks down. God obviously does not have to earn a living; he does not support a particular football team. The same sort of thing applies when we speak of God as the Creator. We are saying that God as the source of all existence is a little like us creating a painting, composing music, a home environment, and so on – but not quite. God creates from nothing; we create by rearranging what already exists. Again, when Christians speak of Christ as the Son of God, or as our Heavenly King, we are saying that these can be helpful ways for conveying a measure of understanding of these relationships, without implying that the father–son and sovereign–subject analogies hold in every respect.

All this is well known. What is not so readily recognized when speaking of the nature of God, is that when we describe him as the God of love, we are again using an analogy. We are saying God's relationship to us is something like the love we might show to another person. But the similarity is unlikely to be exact. Thus we cannot legitimately argue that, just because our type of love might inhibit us from putting someone else through some kind of trial, God's type of love would similarly prohibit it.

With our type of love for fellow humans, as we have seen, it begins with the wish to promote the other person's happiness. But if this leads to a mother always giving in to the short-term wishes of her child, regardless of the possible longer-term consequences, then this is no longer love but indulgence. True love cannot be solely centred on the promotion of happiness here and now. The priority has to be what is ultimately best for the other. For this reason, the good mother insists on unwelcome discipline over such matters as cleaning teeth, cutting down on the intake of sugar, doing homework – all this in the face of uncomprehending protests from the child. So if this is how love in action is modified as a result of seeing life in a longer-term context, might we not expect that from God's even wider transcendental perspective an even higher form of love might lead to yet further unexpected, and from our limited point of view seemingly incomprehensible, outcomes? Let me repeat: in claiming that God is a God of love, we are simply drawing an analogy between Divine love and our ordinary human type of love. The analogy is not exact. Certainly it does not follow that the existence of evil and suffering rules out a God of love. It depends on how one defines 'love'.

Another attribute of God is that he is held to be a God of justice. But is life just? One has only to consider the various life experiences of people to realize that it manifestly is not. Compare, for example,

155

the comfortable lifestyle of an American or European middle-class person with that of a refugee fleeing a war-torn, famine-ravaged African nation. Where does a God of justice fit in with this picture? That is the subject of the next section.

Death and eternal life

The unfairness of life depends on one big assumption, namely that this earthly life is all that there is. But that is not the case according to the world's major religions. This life is but part of the overall picture. There is a kind of existence that extends beyond the one we presently experience. There are disagreements between the religions as to what exactly that other life consists of: heaven and hell, nirvana, reincarnation, and so on. But there is one thing they do agree about, and that is that the quality of that other life is dependent on the kind of life we live in the here and now. It is only in this way that the manifold injustices of this life have a chance of being put right. Belief in an eternal life becomes indispensable to belief in a God of justice and, indeed, to belief in a God of love.

Of course there will be those who dismiss the idea of life beyond death as nothing more than a vain hope for 'pie in the sky when you die'. Sigmund Freud put it down to wish fulfilment. But one of the problems with dismissing it as wish fulfilment is that none of the great Old Testament figures fell prey to it. Here we have in mind Abraham, Isaac, Jacob, Moses, Isaiah, Jeremiah and Ezekiel. Presumably they would have wished for it as much as we. But for most of Old Testament times there was no belief in resurrection, just a vague belief in a kind of existence called Sheol, probably meaning 'non-land' or 'un-land'. It was held to be a closed space under the disc of the Earth. It was a place of darkness and silence where one was condemned to a ghostlike existence. A mere shadow of one's former self, one was incapable of interacting with other people or with God. Hardly something to be wished for! According to those earlier beliefs, one lived on only in one's surviving kin, hence the importance of having children to carry on the line. Acceptance that there was a personal life beyond, and moreover that it might be something to be desired, was a late development. In the Bible one finds it for the first time in the book of

Daniel, dated around 165 BCE, and it culminates in the teachings of Jesus and the claim that he himself underwent resurrection.

So we can set aside the assertion (for that is all it is) that belief in life beyond the grave is mere wish fulfilment. Even so, is such a belief tenable? When gazing at a dead body, or at a skeleton, or the ashes resulting from a cremation, it is hard to escape the conclusion that this marks the end of that person. We are all too aware that the conscious self is intimately bound up with what goes on in the physical body, and especially in the brain. It would, therefore, appear but logical to accept that when the body is destroyed, and there is no longer a brain, consciousness must die with it.

But are we in fact being logical? Such a conclusion rests on an important assumption – one that goes largely unacknowledged. We are assuming that over the course of evolution, as the human brain became ever more complicated and sophisticated in its structure and workings, this complexity led to the brain becoming conscious. Consciousness is regarded as being a natural outgrowth of the physical complexity. In other words, consciousness is a by-product of biology. It is the biology that causes consciousness. Take away the biological basis and consciousness has no independent existence.

However, such an interpretation does have its difficulties. First, we need to recognize that no one – and I mean absolutely no one – has the slightest understanding as to how consciousness is supposed to emerge out of something that is physical. As was pointed out earlier, there have been attempts, but none has succeeded in supplying a mechanism by which one gives rise to the other. Claiming that biology gives rise to consciousness when there is a complete absence of any explanation as to how this comes about becomes a matter of faith rather science.

We have here a classic problem often encountered in the medical and social sciences: confusion over correlation and causation. In the present discussion there is no doubt that for the type of consciousness we know about there is a correlation between it and a physical human body. Sure enough, if you take a paracetamol it is accompanied by the mental sensation of relief from pain. Likewise, damage to the brain due to a stroke can be accompanied by a loss of cognitive ability. But is that correlation correctly to be regarded as a causal one?

I recall, for example, the result of a survey that clearly demon-strated a correlation between coffee drinking and heart disease. The more coffee you drank, the greater your chance of having heart prob-lems. The blame lay with the caffeine contained in coffee. On reading this news report I and many others promptly took the advice doctors were giving at the time and switched to decaffeinated coffee – even though I did not really like it. This went on for years. But then further investigations, carried out with greater care, revealed that the uptight, stressed kind of person who habitually drinks lots of coffee was also likely to be a heavy smoker. This had been overlooked. Later surveys that carefully controlled for the smoking habit demonstrated that it was not the caffeine that was responsible for the increased heart disease but the accompanying habit of smoking. In fact one could drink six cups of coffee a day with no ill effects should one so wish. Certainly the disease was correlated to the caffeine, but the connec-tion was incidental; it was not causal. Needless to say, I am back to drinking proper coffee again!

This kind of confusion is common. In the case of the brain and consciousness, there is an absence of any known mechanism by which the physical brain can be understood to give rise to consciousness. Indeed, how can something physical be responsible for the produc-tion of something that is so different in nature from itself that it requires an entirely different language to describe it?

In the philosophy of science, data is often referred to as being 'theory-laden'. This idea holds that as one approaches one's observa-tions of the world, one's mind is not a blank waiting to absorb objective facts. Instead one already entertains some theory or has a particular mindset, and this affects how one interprets the observations.

The neuroscientist's prime concern is with the workings of the brain. It is not surprising, then, on finding a certain pattern of brain activity to be accompanied by a certain mental process, that she interprets the situation as the brain process having caused the mental process. Without the brain activity, there would not have been the changed mental state.

However, on leaving the laboratory and making her way home she now adopts a different mindset. The question arises as to whether she will go home by bus or train; should she stop on the way to buy something for dinner; what in fact will she decide to have for dinner that night; which television programmes will she choose to watch; should she have an early night . . .? One decision after another. The physical/mental situation has been reversed. She is no longer concerned with the mechanics of how the brain works, but is getting on with the business of living her day-to-day life. It is now a case of mental decisions being made and these leading to the appropriate physical actions. Thus, contrary to what we were earlier saying, it is the mental state that has caused the physical action.

Thus the whole question of causation is intimately bound up with the mindset one has adopted. For the neuroscientist in the laboratory, what matters are brain processes – conscious experience being a mere epiphenomenon. On the other hand, for most of us, most of the time, what matters is living out one's day-to-day life – the physical world being merely a medium through which the mind achieves its aims and objectives through controlling the actions of the body.

And not just controlling the body in general, but the brain in particular. Just now we said that changes to the brain state brought about by taking paracetamol causes the mental headache to be cured. But equally we could have said that it was the mental decision to take the paracetamol that led to the changed brain state.

It has been shown that brain training with simple games conducted online can cut the risk of dementia by a third. Brain scans show that if one engages in repeated mental exercises, such as the practice of meditation, this leads to the building of new neuronal circuits. The more the activity is repeated, the stronger these new circuits become. As we have said, in these instances the natural interpretation of what is going on is that it is the focused mental attention that is the cause of the changed brain states, and not the other way round.

To sum up, all we can be sure about is that there is a correlation between what goes on in the brain and what goes on in the mind. The question of which causes which, or whether one can occur without the other, is much more contentious. Certainly there is no justification for asserting that the only way of interpreting the data is to claim that consciousness is caused by biology, and hence, without an ongoing biological basis, there cannot be consciousness, and thus there cannot be eternal life beyond the death of the physical brain.

An alternative way of looking at the problem is to say that if we are to bring causation into the discussion, then it is not biology that is the cause of consciousness but God – God being defined as the source of all existence. As we have noted, God is not only the source of the physical world but also of consciousness. Consciousness ultimately owes its existence to God, not to biology.

That being so, who is to say God cannot take consciousness, as shaped in conjunction with the physical body, and give it a further type of existence divorced from the physical? Admittedly it is difficult for us to envisage a consciousness divorced from a physical body, and in particular its brain. But the consciousness of God does not require it to be associated with a physical body. Our consciousness is derived from the conscious aspect of God – a chip off the old block, so to speak – so why should not God be able to transpose it to an altogether different, non-physical, realm of existence – heaven or whatever? The physical life we lead can then be regarded merely as a 'vale of soul-making', as the poet John Keats put it. Or, to express it another way, our physical life is merely a mould through which our spiritual selves are shaped and take form, a mould that can subsequently be broken at death because by then the soul can be endowed with an independent type of existence.

But what exactly is God going to resurrect? Christians speak of the resurrection of the body. This can lead to confusion. It does not mean that the decayed remnants of the dead body are to be reassembled to form an intact body once more. It is a statement meant to convey the idea that we shall preserve our individuality, rather than being absorbed into some kind of anonymous spiritual soup.

The common view, I suppose, is that God resurrects us as the kind of person we are at the time of death, one's younger self having passed into oblivion. Which, if true, is surely a pity. How many die with Alzheimer's disease or a host of other disabilities mental and physical? Is that what God is to perpetuate? What if God preferred us as we used to be earlier in life, before we might have become somewhat world-weary, disillusioned, cynical, and so on?

There is an alternative. The theologian Franz-Josef Nocke wrote: 'Bodily resurrection means that a person's life history and all the relationships established in the course of his history enter together in the consummation and finally belong to the risen person.' Another theologian, Wilhelm Breuning, agrees: 'Resurrection of the body means that in God man rediscovers not only his last moment but his history.' Likewise, Hans Küng claims: 'What matters is the identity of the person. The question arises then of the permanent importance of my whole life and lot.'

Some might find it difficult to accept that events which have long ago ceased could somehow be brought back into existence in this manner. Surely, it might be argued, when I die all that exists is how I am at that particular point in time. My present form has replaced the earlier versions of me. It is a logical impossibility to have all versions of me, and everything that has ever happened to me, all existing together.

But no, it is not a logical impossibility. Or at least it is not according to one widely held interpretation of physics. Recall our earlier discussion of Einstein's ideas about space and time and how they are to be seen as but projections of a four-dimensional reality named spacetime. We saw that spacetime, otherwise known as the block universe, consists of all the events that have ever happened, are happening and are yet to happen according to our normal perception of events occurring sequentially in time. It all exists on an equal footing. In particular, all the events that make up our lives, from birth to death, are etched permanently into this four-dimensional existence. It is called our *world line.*

Earlier we discussed the block universe in the context of God being able to possess foreknowledge. From a position that is somehow 'outside' of spacetime – in a still higher dimension, so to speak – he can take it all in at once. Now we examine spacetime to see whether it can throw any light on eternal life and resurrection. According to relativity theory, the whole of our world line exists. Moreover, it exists eternally. We pointed out that spacetime cannot exist in time; rather, time is incorporated into spacetime. So acceptance of the notion of spacetime is indeed acceptance also that it makes sense to think of this block of space and time existing as an entity suspended in some higher form of dimensionality – one that is transcendent, eternal, beyond time. And if this is the case, what is true of spacetime as a whole must also be true in particular of our world line. There is nothing more truly you or me than our world line – it incorporates the totality of our life. And there it is, existing in this eternal arena.

That being the case, why resurrect us as we happen to be at the very end point of our world line when spacetime offers God access to the whole of our life, with our childhood as vividly present to him as any other feature of our history? So perhaps, in some sense entirely beyond our comprehension, resurrection applies to the whole of our world line, not just to its end point.

Earlier we spoke of the searchlight beam of consciousness sweeping sequentially along the world line from birth to death. Perhaps when that is switched off at the point of death, we become more acutely aware of an ever-present type of conscious experience associated with the totality of our world line. After all, it is commonly held by theologians that eternal life is not something that will happen to us later after death; we are already embarked upon it in this life. One of the conventional phrases a priest might say over someone receiving Holy Communion is 'The body of Christ keep you in eternal life.' Note the word 'keep'. Perhaps through those qualities of consciousness that are hard to explain as belonging to the mind of a self-replicating survival machine we are already experiencing this transcendent type of consciousness – that of which we shall be more vividly aware when the distractions and demands of ordinary consciousness are stilled at death.

But enough of speculation – for that is all it is: the idiosyncratic musings of a physicist. Let us turn to a topic that is more grounded: what actual evidence might there be for life beyond death, particularly for the Christian idea of resurrection?

To begin with, we ask what we are to make of accounts given by people claiming to have come back from the dead. We are told how they had experiences of passing through a tunnel into a blinding light, or floating out of their body and looking down on it lying in the hospital bed, visions of their physical body being linked by a silver umbilical cord to a spiritual body, encounters with orbs, feelings of joy and peace, and so on. These are called near-death experiences, and that is what they are: *near*-death experiences. The whole subject of how one is to define death is a contentious one. Certainly it can be identified with the irreversible stoppage of all vital functions, but how is that to be determined? The heart stopping, breath stopping, brain inactivity, or what? There have been innumerable examples of people being resuscitated from such conditions, so they were not really dead. And the same applies to all those reporting near-death experiences: they might have been close to dying, but they did not actually die. Indeed, one does not even have to be close to death to have such experiences. They can be triggered, for example, by stress, depression, emotional crises or meditation.

As for deathbed visions, these are occasions when someone who is close to death, often a resident in a hospice, speaks of being visited by dead relatives or angels who have come to accompany them to the next life. It is not easy to account for such occurrences, but one thing is clear: they are not in themselves a first-hand experience of a life beyond.

Which brings us to the reported resurrection of Jesus. How reliable are we to regard the accounts of that?

First, we note that we can surely discount any claim that he did not really die. He was crucified; he had a sword thrust into his side; he was in the tomb for three days. So having died, we can take it that coming back to life again would have required a miracle – a miracle in what we have been calling the narrow sense, meaning it must have involved a violation of the normal laws of nature. Consequently, reminding ourselves of the various reservations we expressed earlier when dealing with law-breaking miracles in general, we are alerted to the need to be on our guard over accepting too easily the accounts of this resurrection as being literally what happened. We know only too well the cavalier approach ancient people had over embellishing stories of wondrous happenings.

However – and it is a big however – close examination of these resurrection accounts reveals that there is a world of difference between this miracle and the others.

In the first place we need to recognize that traditional Jewish miracle stories were invariably written to a pattern. Each was divided into three parts. The first part sets the scene. For a typical healing miracle it would describe the condition of the person to be cured in sufficient detail to indicate that it really would take a miracle to bring about a cure. So, for example, the man was born blind; it was not some temporary blindness. Then comes the main part of the story, the account of the miracle itself, complete with accompanying words and actions. Thus the blind man has mud put on his eyes and he is told to go and wash them. Finally, the last part describes the reaction of the onlookers; they are utterly astonished, demonstrating that this was indeed an amazing event.

How do the accounts of the resurrection conform to this pattern? The first part of the story is there – all the events leading up to the crucifixion: the Last Supper, Jesus' betrayal, his trial and torture, his death, his burial and the guards put in place outside his tomb. The third part of the story is there: his subsequent appearances on various occasions to the women and to the disciples, the words he spoke to them, his invitation to doubting Thomas to put his hand into the wound caused by the sword and his fingers into the marks of the nails, the general expressions of astonishment and delight on the part of those who witnessed the risen Jesus. So we have in place two of the components of a traditional Jewish miracle story.

But where is the middle section – the all-important part that describes the actual miracle itself, complete with accompanying actions and words? It is not there. It is entirely missing. Why? Scholars tell us that it is unthinkable for a Jewish miracle story to be composed in such a form. One can judge just how scandalous this was deemed to be by examining the accounts in the order in which they were written. In doing so we find the writers progressively trying to fill in the missing details. Beginning with the earliest of the Gospels, Mark describes the empty tomb with the stone that was originally in front of the entrance rolled away. The women enter the tomb and find it empty apart from a young man in a white robe who tells them that Jesus has risen. And that's it; there are no further details. (Here we are referring to the most reliable early manuscripts of the Gospel, which do not have the additional verses, Mark 16.9–20.) In Matthew's later Gospel we are told that this man was an angel – an identification perhaps helped by the fact that in the first century angels were not thought to have wings. Instead of the tomb already being open, Matthew describes the angel descending and rolling away the stone that was blocking the entrance, to the accompaniment of an earthquake. By the time we get to Luke and John, the angel has been joined by a second one, their clothes 'gleaming like lightning'.

Thus we see the first attempts to cover the embarrassing lack of details of the miracle with some legendary additions. But these elaborations are as nothing compared to what we read in the apocryphal *Gospel of Peter*. Starting from Matthew's modest additions, the writer of this Gospel describes how two men, encircled by a great light, descend and rolled the stone away. Three men come out of the tomb, two supporting the third. The heads of the two reach as far as heaven, but the head of the third overtops the heavens. They are followed by a cross. A voice from heaven intones, 'Hast thou preached to them that sleep?' A voice from the cross pronounces, 'Yea.'

All of which is so far-fetched it is no surprise this Gospel was not accepted for inclusion in the Bible. Nevertheless, the account does neatly illustrate just how shocking the missing second section of the original version was to Jewish sensibilities. Subsequent writers felt compelled to add something to plug the gap in the narration.

So how are we to account for the original missing section? The most straightforward explanation is that this was never meant as an ordinary Jewish miracle story to be added to all the others. It was a description of what actually happened. The reason the middle section is missing is that no one was around to witness at first hand how the resurrection occurred.

Examining the accounts in more detail reveals that they have all the hallmarks of being authentic eyewitness descriptions of what actually happened. In the first place, such accounts are unlikely to follow a structured logical sequence of the key points that need to be got across. Often you get inconsequential details that add nothing useful to the narration but are included simply because that is what happened. Thus we learn that two disciples ran to the tomb; the one who got there first did not go straight in but, for some unknown reason, waited for the other to come, and it was the latter who went in first. Who cares? One feels like protesting, 'For goodness sake, get to the point.' But it is included because that is the way it was.

Another feature of eyewitness accounts is that moments of shock are recalled particularly vividly. The witness is describing something that is still etched in their mind's eye. Thus when the disciples enter the tomb they are shocked to find it empty. The scene stamps itself on their memory. They describe how the cloth that was over Jesus' face was lying a little apart from the other clothes. A minor detail is mentioned only because they are in a sense describing a picture that is still before them in all its detail.

With real eyewitness accounts there can be features of one's own behaviour which, embarrassingly, one finds difficult to explain. A familiar phrase is, 'I simply don't know what came over me.' Thus we find Mary Magdalene meeting the risen Jesus in the garden outside the tomb and, for some unaccountable reason, not recognizing him but mistaking him for the gardener. Recognition only came when he spoke her name. This was of special significance for Mary. She had been a prostitute; men had treated her as a nameless sex object. But to Jesus she was not an anonymous object but someone to be respected and whose name was Mary. To be so addressed doubtless meant a lot to her.

The same sort of thing happened with the two followers of Jesus who, on being joined by the risen Jesus on the road to Emmaus, also did not recognize him. It was only when they were indoors having a meal and he broke bread with them that 'their eyes were opened'. Why was the breaking of bread a trigger for recognition? These followers had not been present at the Last Supper but might well on occasion have had other meals with him. In any case, they would doubtless have heard the report of Jesus breaking bread the night he was betrayed and startling his hearers with the declaration that this was his body that they had to eat.

What alternative explanation can we have for the empty tomb? The priests at that time put around the story that the disciples must have stolen the body and made up the story of a resurrection. But why would they have done such a thing? Was it a last-ditch attempt to claim that, despite the disgrace and humiliation of dying the death of a criminal on the cross, Jesus was, nevertheless, the long-awaited Messiah? No. That cannot have been the reason because there had never been any expectation that the Messiah would undergo a resurrection.

Not only that but, if there had been such a conspiracy, wouldn't the disciples have taken the trouble to get their story straight? Their accounts do not tie up. Matthew and Mark, for example, hold that Jesus' resurrection appearances took place exclusively in Galilee. Luke describes them as taking place in or around Jerusalem. John has them occurring in both locations. Why the discrepancies? The most reasonable conclusion is that we are not dealing with a cunningly concocted story designed to deceive, but with various genuine, but sometimes faulty attempts to describe what actually happened. Eyewitness accounts are well known to be liable to have this further feature of being inconsistent. It is when schoolboys troop into the head teacher's office and parrot identical stories about the fight in the playground that one suspects collusion.

In any case, what possible motive could the disciples have had for making up such a story? Immediately after the crucifixion of Jesus we read how the disciples were in hiding 'for fear of the Jews'. They daren't show their faces. And if they had dared to go out, what would their message have been? Not a silly story that he had come back to life again; no one was likely to take that seriously. In all probability it would have been to declare outrage at the gross injustice of a perfectly innocent man being wrongly accused and put to a shameful death. There is no more potent a rallying call than protesting the death of a martyr. But that was not what happened. Once they had got over their initial shocked reaction to Jesus' death, we find them fearlessly out in the streets, not in protest at injustice but joyfully proclaiming a great victory. From then on they risked the wrath of the authorities and even martyrdom for themselves with the claim that Jesus had risen.

Indeed, the strongest evidence for the resurrection does not consist of arguments in favour of an empty tomb, but the dramatic transformation in the behaviour of Jesus' followers. Something quite exceptional must have brought it about.

It is not for nothing that the very first accounts of the resurrection – not Mark's Gospel, but the letters of Paul – do not tell us anything about an empty tomb but concentrate exclusively on Jesus' appearances to his followers. For Paul the most important message he wanted to get across was the profound impact that the risen Jesus made on his followers, including the life-changing impact Jesus had on Paul himself through his own vision on the road to Damascus.

Summing up, one can say that, although many will remain so convinced of the finality of death they are unwilling or unable to accept Jesus' resurrection, there is no getting away from the fact that the accounts we have of it could not appear more authentic than they are.

Learning from other people

We have been examining the physical world to see whether it provides confirmatory evidence of the kind of God we appear to encounter through the otherness of our conscious experience. Probably the most important feature of that world is the presence of other human beings. This opens up a potentially fruitful new line of enquiry.

In getting to know God we have so far had to rely on what we have found in our own individual consciousness. But other people are also conscious. We can therefore explore whether their observations lead to the same sort of conclusions we have arrived at as to the nature of God. Indeed, it might turn out that they have been more perceptive and wise than ourselves in the interpretation of conscious experience. That being so, as with other areas of knowledge, we might learn from them. Knowledge is shared; we no longer have to go it alone.

What one finds is that, although there is no unanimity over the findings, vast numbers of people do indeed report the same type of experiences regarding getting to know God in this manner. So what are we to make of this?

One sometimes hears of there being a clear distinction between scientific and theological inquiry. Science is objective, theology subjective. With a scientific investigation we can jointly examine some physical phenomenon set out before us. We can agree over what we see happening, and arrive at a consensus as to what the explanation of it might be. When examining consciousness, however, one has access only to one's own mind. We cannot jointly examine the same consciousness. So we are not working with the same objective data. We are engaged in separate private enterprises rather than a single venture.

Except that the distinction between the scientific and theological enterprises need not be as clear-cut as sometimes assumed. In my scientific work I find I am not in fact always examining the same data as some other scientist. It is more likely that I will conduct an experiment in my laboratory and the other scientist will repeat a similar experiment in his or her laboratory. I collect my set of data and the other scientist collects his or hers. It is these two sets of data, drawn from separate experiments, that we compare. More often than not a scientific theory is confirmed not by scientists examining a single set of data, but by repeating the experiment, often under somewhat different circumstances to see if the results really are reproducible. That does not seem to me to be all that different from me comparing what I find in my consciousness with what you find in yours. And if we find the same feature present in both, then we are on to something that is objective and not some peculiar subjective quirk of an individual mind.

So it is we look to other people to learn more than can be gathered from one's own direct experience of life. We prize particularly the insights of holy people gathered over the ages and set down in the Bible, the Qur'an and other holy writings.

We have just been examining an example of this. We saw, concerning the question of resurrection, that we can do our best to weigh up in our own mind the pros and cons of whether it is reasonable to believe in a life beyond this one. But ultimately the clearest indication comes from considering the experience of someone else, namely Jesus. Indeed, for Christians, Jesus was so transparent to the will of God – so in tune with the otherness of the mind as imprinted by God – that he was the perfect conduit for God to reach out to others. Though we might see something of God in those we meet from day to day, and this can be valuable, such revelations of God are always clouded by human imperfections. Jesus, according to Christians, was free of all such imperfections. Meeting up with him was in effect meeting up with God directly.

Thus communing with others and sharing insights becomes an integral part of enriching one's understanding of God. In particular, we learn by mixing with fellow believers in the religious community to which we belong. It is not for nothing that one of Jesus' first acts on embarking on his ministry was to gather a band of followers who could be of mutual help to each other. He instituted Holy Communion in the knowledge that this would ensure that they would keep together. He sent out his disciples in pairs, rather than alone, to carry out missionary work. He founded his Church on Peter. For Jesus, religion was not restricted to being but a private matter between the individual and God. If we are to enrich our understanding of God, we need to look to the world and especially to each other.

Epilogue

So ends our journey exploring the roots of belief in God. We have seen that getting to know God was primarily a matter of coming to terms with what one finds imprinted in the depths of consciousness. We were mistaken in trying first to find him through a scientific study of the physical world. Only having got to know God through introspection is one sensitized to the marks of God's imprint on the world.

Given this to be the case, one might well ask why so much has been written about the relationship between religious belief and the sciences. Each year sees the publication of book after book based on the arguments we have earlier summarized – all centred on what one finds in the physical world. Richard Dawkins's book *The God Delusion*, claiming to have done away with God on scientific grounds, became a bestseller. Stephen Hawking was equally dismissive of theology in his popular book *The Grand Design*. In it he declares philosophy also to be dead, and that in our time 'scientists have become the bearers of the torch of discovery in our quest for knowledge'.

I myself have written books and given countless talks on the subject. I have been involved in public debates about these issues with atheists such as Dawkins. But why? If the study of the physical and biological world, by its very nature, is incapable of supplying cast-iron proof of a personal God, what are we all arguing about?

Speaking for myself, I believe no one ever gets argued into a belief in God. It is not like that. However, there are these writers who argue the opposite – that on the basis of science, the weight of evidence *dis*-proves the existence of God. It is that last step that is false and needs to be countered. While agreeing that science cannot prove the existence of God, neither can it disprove belief in God. It is this misleading impression that needs to be challenged.

As just noted, books written from this atheistic point of view receive a lot of attention – despite being written by those who, though highly qualified in their own scientific field, often know little or nothing about modern theology. Books written in refutation of these views, by those properly qualified to talk on theological matters, never seem to make it on to the bestseller list. Neither do these informed contributions get an airing in the media. The media has a vested interest in stoking up controversy. It is good for increasing viewing and listening figures and boosting the circulation of newspapers. 'God is dead' makes a good headline. 'God is alive and still in charge' does not. One understands why the bias is there. Unfortunately the public thereby is denied a proper, well-balanced discussion of the issues.

It is because of this that I have considered it important to engage in the debate. As far as I am concerned, our initial study of science was in effect telling us to go and look for God in some more appropriate way. Only then should we come back and take a fresh look at the world, this time having a better idea of the signs we should be seeking. This I have tried to do.

References

Works referred to or quoted from in the text:

4 Paul Tillich, *Systematic Theology, Vol. 1*, Chicago, IL: University of Chicago Press, 1973.

4 Hans Küng, *Does God Exist?* London: Collins, 1978, p. 544.

12 Christina Rossetti, *Sing-Song: A Nursery Rhyme Book*, London: George Routledge, 1872.

30 Stephen Hawking and Leonard Mlodinow, *The Grand Design*, London: Bantam Press, 2010.

40 Dan Dennett, *Consciousness Explained*, London: Penguin, 1991.

42 Augustine, *Confessions*, London: Penguin Classics, 2002.

42 Blaise Pascal, *Pensées*, London: Penguin Classics, 1995.

42 Gregory Palamas, *The Triads*, Classics of Western Spirituality, New York: Paulist Press, 1983.

45 Thomas Aquinas, *De Veritate*, question 2, article 3.19.

51 Francis Crick, *The Astonishing Hypothesis: The Scientific Search for the Soul*, New York: Touchstone, 1995.

51 Edward O. Wilson, *Consilience: The Unity of Knowledge*, London: Abacus, 1998.

70 David Hume, *A Treatise of Human Nature*, Book III, Part I, Section I, London: Penguin Classics, 1985.

81 Charles Darwin, *On The Origin of Species*, Wordsworth Classics of World Literature, London: Wordsworth, 1998.

109 Carl Gustav Jung, *Modern Man in Search of a Soul*, London: Routledge Classics, 2001.

110 Sigmund Freud, *The Future of an Illusion*, London: Penguin, 2011.

110 Sigmund Freud, *Moses and Monotheism*, London: Aziloth Books, 2013.

110 Sigmund Freud, *Totem and Taboo*, London: Routledge Classics, 2001.

139 Hermann Minkowski, 'Space and Time', in Hendrik A. Lorentz, Albert Einstein, Hermann Minkowski and Hermann Weyl, *The Principle of Relativity: A Collection of Original Memoirs on the Special and General Theory of Relativity*, New York: Dover, 1952, p. 75.

147 Simon Conway Morris, *Life's Solution*, Cambridge: Cambridge University Press, 2003.

149 Carl Gustav Jung, *The Red Book*, ed. S. Shamdasani, New York and London: Norton & Co., 2009.

160 John Keats, Letter to his brother George and sister Georgiana (1819).

160 Franz-Josef Nocke, *Eschatologie*, Düsseldorf: Patmos Verlag, 1982, p. 123.

161 Wilhelm Breuning, in J. Feiner and M. Löhrer (eds), *Mysterium Salutis*, vol. V, Einsiedeln: Benziger Verlag, 1976, p. 882.

161 Hans Küng, *Eternal Life?* London: SCM Press, 1984, p. 111.

171 Richard Dawkins, *The God Delusion*, London: Bantam Press, 2006.

171 Stephen Hawking and Leonard Mlodinow, *The Grand Design*, London: Bantam Press, 2010, p. 5.

Further reading

For comprehensive accounts of evolutionary psychology:

Jerome H. Barkow, Leda Cosmides and John Tooby (eds), *The Adapted Mind: Evolutionary Psychology and the Generation of Culture*, Oxford: Oxford University Press, 1992.

David M. Buss, *Evolutionary Psychology: The New Science of the Mind*, Boston, MA: Allyn & Bacon, 2004.

David M. Buss (ed.), *The Handbook of Evolutionary Psychology*, Hoboken, NJ: Wiley, 2005.

An evolutionary psychologist's attempt to explain away religiosity by invoking a theory of mind:

Jesse Bering, *The God Instinct: The Psychology of Souls, Destiny and the Meaning of Life*, London: Nicholas Brealey Publishing, 2011.

For a balanced approach to the development of religion:

Nicholas Wade, *The Faith Instinct: How Religion Evolved and Why It Endures*, New York: Penguin, 2009.

Accounts of Jungian psychology:

Carl Gustav Jung, *Memories, Dreams, and Reflections*, London: Flamingo, 1995.

Anthony Storr, *The Essential Jung: Selected Writings*, London: Fontana, 1973.

A neuroscientist's approach to religious experiences:

Mario Beauregard and Denyse O'Leary, *The Spiritual Brain: A Neuroscientist's Case for the Existence of the Soul*, New York: HarperOne, 2007.

The free-will problem as seen from a neuroscientist's perspective:

Peter Clarke, *All in the Mind: Does Neuroscience Challenge Faith?* Oxford: Lion Hudson, 2015.

Neuroscientists taking the view that mental states cause brain processes:

Andrew Newberg and Mark Robert Waldman, *How God Changes Your Brain*, New York: Ballantine Books, 2010.

Further reading

Scholarly essays on the cognitive science of religion:

Fraser Watts and Léon Turner (eds), *Evolution, Religion and Cognitive Science: Critical and Constructive Essays*, Oxford: Oxford University Press, 2014.

There are many books on various approaches to the relationships between science and religion. Here is a short selection:

Ian Barbour, *Religion in an Age of Science*, London: SCM Press, 1990.

Paul Davies, *The Mind of God: Science and the Search for Ultimate Meaning*, London: Simon & Schuster, 1992.

Mary Midgley, *Beast and Man*, London: Routledge, 2002.

John Polkinghorne, *Reason and Reality: The Relationship between Science and Theology*, London: SPCK, 1991.

W. Mark Richardson, Robert J. Russell, Philip Clayton and Kirk Wegter-McNelly (eds), *Science and the Spiritual Quest: New Essays by Leading Scientists*, London: Routledge, 2002.

Russell Stannard, *The God Experiment*, London: Faber & Faber, 1999.

Keith Ward, *The Evidence for God: The Case for the Existence of the Spiritual Dimension*, London: Darton, Longman & Todd, 2014.

Index

Abraham 137, 156

Adam 2, 21, 120, 145

adaptations 47, 50–1, 71, 73, 82, 91, 94, 96, 111, 115

altruism 58–69, 115; on behalf of close kin 61, 68–9, 115; reciprocal 61–4, 68–9, 113, 115

Amos 117

anthropic principle 24–7, 29, 131

archetypes 111–14, 149

argument from design *see* design, argument from

Arp, Jean 74

Augustine, St 11, 32–3, 42

awareness 19, 40, 52–3, 96, 101, 104–5, 116, 121, 140, 162

awe, sense of 83–4, 101, 103–4, 107, 114–15, 119, 132–3

beauty, sense of 71–82, 104, 107, 115, 123, 133–4; in art 74–7, 86, 119; as a by-product 82–3; in literature 77–8; in math- ematics and science 81–2; in music 78–80, 116, 119; in nature 80–1; sexual 71–5, 115

behaviour *see* competitive behaviours; genetically determined behaviour; genetically influenced behaviour

belief, roots of 7, 17, 30, 34, 116–24, 171

Bible 2, 5, 14–16, 29, 45, 118, 129, 137, 142, 156, 165, 169

Big Bang 2, 24, 30, 32, 133, 138

Big Crunch 25

block universe 140–1, 161

brain, modular structure of 47, 85

Breuning, Wilhelm 161

Bruckner, Anton 80

causation 30–2, 52, 134, 138, 157–60

CERN laboratory 138

cheaters 62–3, 68, 91

co-creators 128–9

cognitive science of religion 89

commandment, greatest 38, 118; *see also* Ten Commandments

communication through the physical 143–5

competitive behaviour 18, 58–60, 63, 72–3, 87, 89, 113, 115

conscience 102, 105

consciousness 39–42, 45, 58, 60, 70, 104–5, 113–16, 120–4, 128, 133, 140, 145, 157, 160–2, 168–71; as an epiphenomenon 39, 52–5, 159; of God 6, 34, 38–9, 41–2, 45, 120–2, 124, 160

Constable, John 75

convergence 147

creation through evolution 145–8

creationism 21–2

creativity, sense of 84–7, 129–30

Crick, Francis 51

critical density 25

Daniel 157

Darwin, Charles 17, 22, 46, 79, 81, 131

Dawkins, Richard 2, 113, 171
death 5, 58, 118–19, 135, 146–7, 156, 159–68
Dennett, Dan 40
Descartes, René 11, 34
design: argument from 17–30, 131–2, 136, 144–7; Intelligent Design 21–3
determinism 53–6
devil 16, 149
DNA 18–19, 21, 65, 68, 100, 111, 122, 136

Earth 3, 22, 25–7, 31, 33, 43, 88, 131, 135, 147, 150, 156
ego 105, 114, 149
Einstein, Albert 32, 138–9, 161
Elijah 117
emergent properties 43
entropy 135
eternal life or afterlife 108, 156, 159–62
evil 70, 118, 123, 148–56; as absence of goodness 148–9
evolution, Darwin's theory of 17–27, 44–5, 131, 145–7; of the eye 22–3
evolutionary psychology 45–52, 60, 66, 69, 73–82, 85–91, 94, 97, 102–5, 110–11, 115–16, 119
Ezekiel 156

feelings 53
Feuerbach, Ludwig 106
free will 54–8, 116, 119, 123, 130, 140, 146, 152–3; argument from 152–3; compatibilist approach to 57; as illusion 54, 57, 119
Freud, Sigmund 105–10, 156

genes 18, 20, 47, 53, 58, 61, 64–5, 69, 72, 75, 87, 94, 100, 112, 146–7

Genesis 2, 118, 120, 134, 145
genetically determined behaviour 19
genetically influenced behaviour 19, 47, 100, 111, 113
God: as all-powerful 101, 148, 150, 153; as Creator 32–3, 116–17, 128, 130, 133–4, 138, 141–6, 154; as father figure 106, 109–10, 118, 154–5; his foreknowledge 137, 140–1, 161; his kind of love 155; as an illusion 91, 99, 102, 110; of justice 4, 106, 146, 155–6; of love 4, 38, 90, 129, 142, 155–6; as Sustainer 33, 120–1; as unknowable 154; *see also* numinous presence of God
God of the gaps 13, 22–3, 98, 127
Golden Calf 98
goodness 4, 95, 123, 148–53
gossip 58–60
gravity, strength of 24–7
Ground of All Being 4, 30–4, 120–4

Hardy, Alister 103
Hawking, Stephen 30, 171
Heisenberg uncertainty principle 55
Hirst, Damien 77
Holocaust 60, 69–70, 123, 149
Hosea 117
Hume, David 70
'hyperactive agent detector device' 95

Ibsen, Henrik 78
id 105
inflation 25
Isaac 156
Isaiah 156

Jacob 156
Jeremiah 107, 118, 130, 137, 156

Jesus 11, 15–17, 29–30, 38, 69, 107, 118, 137, 142–3, 154, 157, 163–70
Jewish miracle stories, nature of 163–5
Jonah 107
Jung, Carl 38, 109–14, 149; *see also* self, Jungian; shadow, Jungian

Kant, Immanuel 4–5, 37–8, 127
Keats, John 160
Küng, Hans 4, 161

laws of nature 4, 6, 13–14, 28, 30, 43, 51, 52–7, 88, 134–7, 141–5, 153, 163
Libet, Benjamin 54
language: acquisition of 49–50, 150; used to describe God 4, 6, 38–41, 49–50, 115, 158
Laplace, Pierre-Simon 14, 41
Large Hadron Collider 138
length contraction 138
life, nature of 20–1, 43–4

M-theory 30–2
Mary Magdalene 166
Maxwell, James Clerk 81
Messiah 166
Milky Way galaxy 133
mind *see* otherness of the mind; theory of mind (ToM)
Minkowski, Hermann 139
miracles, 14–17, 141–3, 163–5
Mondrian, Piet 77
Monet, Claude 76, 131
moral sense 4, 65, 69–71, 90–1, 104, 115, 118–19, 123, 149
Morris, Simon Conway 147
Moses 29, 107, 110, 130, 156
Mother Teresa 123
Muhammad 29–30

multiverse 28–9, 131–2

nature *see* laws of nature
near-death experiences 162–3
neurons 46, 159
Nocke, Franz-Josef 160
numinous presence of God 100–2, 107, 114, 123, 132–3

opposites, definition by means of 149–50
order and disorder 81, 134–7
original sin 123–4
otherness of the mind 114–16, 119, 123, 127–31, 168–9

pain 40–1, 53, 68, 118, 151–2
Palamas, St Gregory 42
Paley, William 17
Pascal, Blaise 42
Paul, St 15, 137, 167
personhood 106, 121
Peter, St 15–16, 137, 165, 170
Pleistocene hunter-gatherers 48–50, 59, 62, 72–3, 80, 84–5, 91, 94–5
Pollock, Jackson 77
prayer 17, 88–9, 101–4, 124, 132, 137
presidential height index 84
process theologians 137
projection, psychological 106, 109
projections of spacetime 139, 161
promiscuity 64, 70–3
psyche 60–2, 72, 99, 114, 123, 127
psychoanalysis 105–6
purpose, sense of 38, 87–9, 96, 99, 104, 115, 118, 129–30

quantum theory 55–7, 137
Qur'an 29, 169

relativity, Einstein's theory of 32, 138–41, 161–2

religion as a commitment
device 89–93
religious drive 88–100, 112–13
religious experiences 102–10, 113–16
Rembrandt van Rijn 76
Renoir, Pierre-Auguste 76
repression 59, 105, 109
resurrection 15, 137, 156–7, 160–9
Rossetti, Christina 12

self, Jungian 114
self-replicating survival
machine 6, 51–2, 57, 102,
115–16, 127, 162
sexual selection 79
Shakespeare, William 78
shadow, Jungian 149
space, creation of 32, 138
spacetime 32, 138–40, 161–2; *see
also* projections of spacetime
spandrels 49–50, 82, 94, 115
spatial dimensions, number of 27
standard social science model 45
stars: carbon formation in 26;
formation and death of 24–7, 133
suffering 4, 38, 90, 107, 129, 146–56
Sun 3, 24–7, 31, 88, 97, 122, 133,
135, 148

superego 105, 107, 109
supernova explosions 27

Ten Commandments 65
Tennyson, Alfred Lord 63
theory-laden data 158–9
theory of mind (ToM) 96–9
Thomas, St 164
Tillich, Paul 4, 120
time: creation of 32–3, 138; dilation
138
timelessness or transcendence 33,
137–41
Tolstoy, Leo 78

unconscious 54, 59, 67, 104–7,
110–14, 122; collective 111, 122
universe 23–8, 30–3, 128–33, 136;
observable 133

Van Gogh, Vincent 131
VMAT2 gene 100

Wilson, Edward O. 51
wish fulfilment 106–9, 156–7
world line 161–2

Yahweh 117